IRREPRESSIBLE

IRREPRESSIBLE
YUKON'S MARTHA BLACK

Enid Mallory

Copyright © 2024 Enid Mallory
Cataloguing data available from Library and Archives Canada
978-0-88839-679-2 [paperback]
978-0-88839-773-7 [epub]

All rights reserved. No part of this publication may be reproduced, stored in a retrieval system or transmitted, in any form or by any means, electronic, mechanical, audio, photocopying, recording, or otherwise (except for copying permitted by Sections 107 and 108 of the U.S. Copyright Law and except for book reviews for the public press), without the prior written permission of Hancock House Publishers. Permissions and licensing contribute to the book industry by helping to support writers and publishers through the purchase of authorized editions and excerpts.
Please visit www.accesscopyright.ca.

Photographs are copyrighted and taken by the author unless otherwise stated.

Printed in South Korea

Cover & Interior Design: S. Peters.

FRONT COVER PHOTO: UNIVERSITY OF WATERLOO ARCHIVES, WA 19-6-6

We acknowledge the support of the Government of Canada through the Canada Book Fund and the Canada Council for the Arts, and of the Province of British Columbia through the British Columbia Arts Council and the Book Publishing Tax Credit.

Hancock House gratefully acknowledges the Halkomelem Speaking Peoples whose unceded, shared and asserted traditional territories our offices reside upon.

Published simultaneously in Canada and the United States by

HANCOCK HOUSE PUBLISHERS LTD.
19313 Zero Avenue, Surrey, B.C. Canada V3Z 9R9
#104-4550 Birch Bay-Lynden Rd, Blaine, WA, U.S.A. 98230-9436
(800) 938-1114 Fax (800) 983-2262
www.hancockhouse.com info@hancockhouse.com

*But often in
the rugged beauty
and quiet of that
wonderful country,
I forgot all about
politics and searched
for wild flowers.*

Contents

11
1898-1903
Over the Chilkoot

49
1904-1916
Dawson High Society

81
1912-1916
First Lady of the Yukon

103
1916-1919
Mother to Yukon Soldiers

127
1921-1957
Yukon–Ottawa Years

155
Bibliography

157
Endnotes

PACKERS ASCENDING SUMMIT OF CHILKOOT PASS.
COPYRIGHT 1898 E. Hegg.

1898-1903
Over the Chilkoot

AN ICONIC GOLD rush photo taken in 1898 shows a black line of men crawling up the white Chilkoot mountain. Among them is a petite woman with bright blue eyes and a saucy set to her jaw, wearing a heavy brown corduroy velvet skirt of "shockingly immodest" length (to keep it out of slush and snow). It is five yards around the bottom, edged with braid. Between the silk lining and the corduroy, it has a layer of buckram. Above that, she wears a Norfolk sealskin jacket and a blouse with a stiff collar, and beneath the skirt, a pair of voluminous silk bloomers that reaches below her knees. On her feet she has high Russian leather boots.

Her party left Dyea at noon the day before to climb the 35 miles over the Chilkoot Pass to Lake Bennett. At first, they followed an easy wagon road; then they were crossing mountain streams on precarious stones or working their way around huge boulders. Nine miles along, they reached Canyon City, a conglomeration of shacks and tents

|| PREVIOUS PAGE: *This photo by E.A. Hegg captures both the forbidding face of the Chilkoot Mountain and the tenacity of those who were after gold. The few women among them included Martha Munger Purdy, Dawson City Museum, 2005.442.14*

Gold-rush stampeders with their goods landed at Dyea. Chilkoot Mountain in the background. Yukon Archives, Anton Vogee fonds 82_271_114.

sheltered by the high canyon walls. Here were horses, dogs, oxen, goats, beasts of burden of all kinds. But most men had used only their backs to carry a 50- to 100-pound load up the mountain, deposit it here, then go back for another load.

The Munger party were among the lucky ones, financed by fathers with money to spare, who could pay packers, usually Tlingits accustomed to the trail, to tote their goods to the top. The Mungers had paid $900 to have their gear deposited at Lake Bennett. They pushed on the three miles from Canyon City to Sheep Camp. Hunters coming here to find mountain sheep gave the camp its name. Now it was a city of shacks and tents and hopeful climbers. From here they could see a gleaming glacier that loomed 3000 feet into the sky, marked by a slow-moving, ascending line of ant-like creatures black against the snow and ice They found shelter from the wind in the Grand Pacific Hotel, which Martha compared to a woodshed. But her bunk, covered with hay, offered a welcome rest, and a hearty breakfast made her think they could face the climb ahead.

For an hour they climbed over the debris of the April avalanche that had killed 68 people. Three more bodies had been found yesterday and were buried under a cairn of stones. Soon they were crossing streams on thin ice or working along ledges where glacial water tumbled down. Martha dared not look down now, as she held on to roots or the odd stunted tree or clawed at rocks as the sun made wet ice more slippery. She heard horses slip and fall off cliffs, saw men collapse under heavy loads. Sometimes the trail became so narrow that one foot could only go behind the other.

In an interview years later, she would remember how, at first, her cousin and brother were horrified by the behaviour of some people on the trail. They had been brought up as gentlemen. "Afterward, during that trip over the pass, they forgot they were gentlemen … And I forgot I was a lady. I learned to use language that no lady ever uses."[1]

Martha is cursing the high buckram collar that chafes her neck, her tight-boned corset, her heavy, swaying skirt, and her bloomers, which she keeps having to hitch up. Her leather boots are perhaps the only wise thing she is wearing, for their elk hide soles often save her on slippery 30-degree slopes.

But now, near the top, sweating, exhausted, terrified of the drop below her, she feels her foot slip and she falls into a crevice. The sharp edge of a rock cuts through one of her leather boots, and her leg throbs with pain. She sits on a slippery rock and sobs.

Her brother, George, at first tries to comfort her but loses patience. They are only ten feet from the top. "For God's sake, Polly," he says, using his pet name for her, " buck up and be a man. Have some style and move on."[2]

Where the Chilkoot and White Mountain passes converged at the windswept summit, two flags marked the boundary between United States and Canada, recently established by the North West Mounted Police. Yukon Archives, Anton Vogee fonds, 87/271 259.

That does it. Furious at George, she climbs to the top and walks triumphantly to the broker's tent at the "top of the world."

But now the wind cuts through her like a knife. She is hungry, cold and feeling faint, and a niggling fear that she has suppressed for weeks is staring her in the face. She may be pregnant.

She begs for a fire and is told that wood here costs two bits a pound. Finally, George relents and says, "Give her a five-dollar fire."

She takes off her boots, washes her wound and pours iodine on it, dries her wet stockings, drinks tea and gets blissfully warm, with an hour of rest. After that, she pushes the terrifying suspicion of pregnancy into a back corner of her mind and carries on. They have to go through Customs now, because they are entering Canada. Here the American woman from Chicago meets her first fine, sturdy specimens of the

North West Mounted Police. Her first favourable impression will stay with her for the rest of her life.

In the early winter months of '98, some 20 men of the North West Mounted Police were ordered to the top of the White Pass to build and inhabit a large cabin to establish the boundary between Canada and the United States. Americans were disputing the boundary line, trying to push it back to the headwaters of the Yukon. Here, in wicked winds at the top of the mountain, the Mounted Police suffered through an incredibly cold winter in order to greet the spring stampede with the flag of Canada flying.

The trail from the summit to Lake Lindeman is, at first, downhill over sharp rocks, but the last two miles through a stunted pine forest are, for Martha, the worst of the whole trip—rocks tearing her boots apart, roots that make her trip and fall, her hands bleeding. At the end of her strength, she begs the men to leave her where she has fallen. George half-carries her most of the last mile, while Captain Spencer hurries ahead to secure a bed for her in the so-called Tacoma Hotel. It was not supposed to be like this. It was supposed to be her husband, Will, not brother George and five other men helping her at the top of the pass.

Martha had begun married life armed with an education in the fine arts of elocution, needlework, and watercolor and china painting. She could make lemon cream pie and she could type. But she knew little about the day-to-day work and worry of being a wife and mother.

She and Will Purdy settled in a house at Walden, on the Rock Island Railway line, about 10 miles from Chicago. The house was a gift from Martha's father. George Munger's business had rebounded after the great Chicago fire. He now owned 72 laundries in several cities, a sugar plantation in the West Indies, and a 2000-acre ranch in Kansas. By 1890, he had built a mansion, now surrounded by fruit trees and catalpas and flowers in bloom. That year, Martha helped her parents plan a giant 25th anniversary party for 40 house guests and 200 guests coming to dinner.

Will worked for his father's Chicago Rock Island and Pacific Railway as assistant paymaster. Financially, their marriage was off to a good start. Ten years later, they had two children, Warren and Donald. Martha had a nanny, which gave her time and energy for work outside her home.

While the rest of their country was falling into an economic depression, Chicago was thriving as thousands of men labored to build the Columbian Exposition, or World's Fair. Martha, too, was caught up in the excitement of the beautiful "White City," with its palaces and domes and enormous wheel invented by a man named Ferris and capable of whirling through the air 2000 people at a time. Her aunt Martha Morse was a friend of Bertha Palmer, president of the Board of Lady Managers. Martha became her errand girl and was included in many of the ceremonies. She was invited into the elegance of the Palmer mansion for social gatherings. She watched Mrs. Palmer drive the golden nail with a silver hammer to open the Women's Building on Dedication Day. She also watched her navigate the inevitable clashes of personality as the fair took shape, learning from her tact and grace.

Her position at the fair let Martha watch landscape architect Frederick Olmstead at work. What he was creating was not conventional flower beds but expanses of wild nature, with lagoons and streams and trees, vines and shrubs set against the blue backdrop of Lake Michigan. His vision made a lasting impression on Martha.

Martha was at the fair on closing day, when Chicago's favourite mayor, Carter Harrison, was shot by a disappointed and delusional supporter. Harrison had been a close friend of Will's father, Warren Purdy. That event canceled the closing ceremonies for the Exposition and was an exclamation mark to the end of the good times the fair had created.

The Exposition had glorified industry and invention and convinced a generation that anything was possible, only to see the city plunged into a pit of economic despair when it ended. Bankers and businessmen shot themselves, factories closed, fathers without work became alcoholics. As winter added to the misery of unemployment and poverty, mothers could not feed their children or afford coal to warm them. Martha volunteered at Hull House, established by the social worker Jane Addams. Jane's settlement house provided impoverished families with food, clothing, education, even nursery schools.

There was trouble for Father Purdy when 2000 Pullman workers went on strike. There was shooting, burning of railway equipment, riots and an explosion on Michigan Avenue. In the empty White City, arsonists burned seven of the palatial buildings. Federal troops arrived in Chicago to establish order.

Despite the unrest, the 1890s were gay years for Martha and Will and the favoured life they lived. There were dinner parties, soirees, plays and musicals, and they loved to ride with a bicycle club on their tandem bicycle.

By the end of the '90s, Martha and George were both restless. In spite of her love for her two little boys, Martha was finding life monotonous, and Will, away from home ten days each month, was probably seeking excitement elsewhere. Martha wrote about the work and care and restrictions of motherhood, and about husbands who might feel neglected. "If they are good-looking as my husband was, they may wander away to more interesting pursuits."[3]

All over America, news of gold in the Yukon was reaching people whose lives had been ruined by the depression, who were jobless, hopeless, sometimes starving. They suddenly had hope. They could go north, find gold, and reclaim their lives. Martha and Will had come through the depression financially unscathed, but they did need some excitement in their lives.

Will's best friend was Eli Gage, whose father, Lyman J. Gage, was vice-president of the First National Bank. For a time, Lyman Gage had also served as president of the Chicago World's Fair, but he resigned as, across America, banks began to fail. His first imperative was to keep his First National Bank afloat. Eli had married Sophy Weare, whose brother, Will Weare, was director of the North American Trading and Transportation Company, operating on the lower Yukon River.

Steamboats on the lower Yukon would play an important part in the gold rush. Before there was a rail link to Whitehorse and boats on the upper Yukon, they plied the 1700 miles from St. Michael's, Alaska, to supply the settlement at Forty Mile and the new tent city rising at Dawson.

Portus B. Weare had been a fur trader who dealt with John Healey at his trading post at Fort Benton, Montana. As the fur trade waned, Weare moved to Chicago and became wealthy trading in grain. One day in the early '90s, John Healey came into his office and plunked a bag of gold dust on his desk. Healey, who now had a fur post at Dyea, Alaska, said the gold came from Forty Mile on the Yukon River. What he wanted from his old fur-trading friend was money to start a riverboat company to serve the stampede of miners he expected would be coming to the Yukon Valley. Together, they formed the North American Transportation and Trading Company, to compete with the longer established Alaska Commercial Company on the Yukon River.

When a Tagish man known as Skookum Jim and George Carmack in 1896 discovered nuggets of gold on Rabbit Creek, which flowed into the Klondike River, prospectors already on the Yukon River made haste to the Klondike's Rabbit Creek (now called Bonanza). They soon found more gold on two other tributaries of the Klondike, Eldorado and Hunker creeks. Healey and Weare, who had seen this coming, were ready to transport the gold out and a stampede of gold-seekers into the region.

Chicago had a circle of wealthy, influential men well-positioned to get involved in a gold rush. Portus B. Weare was one of them. So was Will's father, Warren G. Purdy, as president of the Rock Island Railroad. So was Eli's father, Lyman J. Gage. Appointed Secretary of the Treasurery in 1897 by President William McKinley, he was instrumental in securing the Gold Standard Act, meant to keep American money backed by gold. Gold was scarce in the 1890s; a gold rush was exactly what was needed.

As rumours of gold reached Chicago in the mid-'90s, Eli, who had been working on the railway with Will, quit his job and went north. He spent the winter in a crude cabin at Circle City on the Lower Yukon. In the spring of 1897, he was working with the North American Trading and Transportation Company for Sophy's brother Will when the *Portus B. Weare* carried her cargo of gold down the Yukon to the sea. Sophy had left her new baby behind to go north with Eli and probably spent the winter at St. Michael's. When the gold was loaded on the *S.S. Portland* bound for Seattle, Sophy was aboard, along with her brother, Will Weare, and 68 grimy, grizzled prospectors, all of them "filthily rich." Among them strode Sophy, dressed in finery and having the time of her life. Interviewed when she landed, she was later quoted in a guide book for fortune seekers, minimizing the hardship and dangers of the Yukon and extolling the ease of getting rich. Back in Chicago, she passed on her enthusiasm to Will and Martha first-hand.

Chicago businessmen considered news from the N.A.T.T. more reliable than secondhand newspaper reports. What they were hearing led to investment and speculation and government lobbying. There was even a scheme to lobby Washington to carve a Yukon River section out of Alaska as a separate territory. With Eli Gage already on the river and his father being Secretary of the Treasury, Eli's name came up as a possible governor of the proposed territory. Nothing came of this scheme.

Will quit his paymaster job. Backed by both fathers, he and Eli formed the Purdy-Gage Company and bought a steamboat, two sailboats and two ocean-going tugs. Ships of all sorts and in every condition were being rushed to the west coast to transport gold-rush stampeders north. Will was making plans to go north with Eli in the spring. Martha watched their great adventure taking shape and begged to go. "I was consumed with the urge to have my part in it."[4] Sophy helped Martha petition their fathers-in-law, who began to think that having their wives along might keep their sons out of trouble.

The matter had not been decided when a man named Lambert came to Father Purdy with a story that his uncle had died in the Klondike and willed his mine plus a million dollars in gold dust to the family. He showed Father Purdy the will, which appeared legitimate, with proper witnesses. If Purdy's son was going to the gold fields, could he act as agent for the family and claim the fortune? Instead, Father Purdy chose Martha for this task. He negotiated with Lambert that her reward should be 50 percent of the gold dust. Martha was delighted with this proposition. She would see the Yukon and she would claim a fortune for her family.

There were serious discussions in the Munger family. George and Susan read the newspapers and the guide books and listened to the talk in Chicago drawing rooms. They knew about the dangers of the Chilkoot Pass, especially after newspapers carried reports of the tragic avalanche in April. Martha and Will would be leaving two small sons behind. But gold fever had infected Martha's parents, too, especially George. He admired Martha's spirit and could not say no to her. He and Susan would care for Warren, aged nine, and Donald, aged three, at Catalpa Knob.

Excitement mounted as brother George and cousin Harry Peachy decided to join Will and Martha. George was six years younger than Martha and had been working in his father's laundry business.

There followed weeks of planning, of gathering more information about the Yukon and how to get there and what equipment was needed and where to find it, now that stampeders were emptying shelves across the country to outfit themselves.

From Catalpa Knob ranch, where Martha said a tearful goodbye to two little boys, she and George and Harry headed to Denver to meet Will and Eli and Sophy Gage. In Denver, they bought clothing for the trip. They were a merry group as they headed to Seattle, where they met the rest of the party: Captain Spencer, business agent for the Purdy-Gage Company, his son Ed, and Captain Treat. The party would split up now, with Eli and Sophy heading south to San Francisco to take a steamboat to St. Michael's, Alaska, then travel the 1700 miles up the Yukon River on one of the Weare boats. The other six would take a ship from Seattle, climb the Chilkoot Pass and find water transportation down the Yukon to Dawson City, where they would all meet.

Martha's euphoria in Seattle was short-lived. Will had a telegram from Eli in San Francisco and had to hurry there on business. Then came a letter that he was delayed there, then another letter, and Martha's world crashed around her.

Will had decided not to go the Klondike. This was the grand adventure that had put new joy into their marriage, that they had planned together all winter. Now he wanted to abort it; he had heard of good opportunities in the Sandwich Islands (Hawaii), and he wanted to go there.

Will argued that she was being unreasonable. He had found a better adventure where they would not freeze to death. He had heard enough about the Chilkoot Pass that he no longer wanted to climb it. Why would she?

Martha asked herself what her mother would do and immediately knew the answer. But Martha was not her mother. There was a family story that makes this clear. Susan Munger was still a teenager when she gave birth to twin girls. George Munger came into the room, looked at the babies and said, "Susan, I'm disappointed. I expected a boy."

The young, exhausted mother said, "Yes, I know. I am so sorry."

Martha later said to her mother, "If my husband had said that to me, I would have thrown those two babies at him."

Her mother's reply was, "Not a man like your dear father."[5]

One of those babies was herself. The other twin did not survive. Martha would always feel the absence of that sister who had shared the womb with her. Perhaps she would need to live larger than life, for the two of them.

Now, Will was suggesting that if she would not come with him, she should go home to her family until he decided what he wanted to do. In her autobiography she writes, "Go to the Sandwich Islands? With my Klondike ticket bought, my passage booked, my vision of a million dollars in gold dust? Even after ten years of married life how little Will Purdy knew me!"[6]

That sentence sums up a marriage that had become shaky. Martha describes this pivotal moment as "the crisis which parted two high-spirited and determined young people."[7] She could not go to the Sandwich Islands with Will. Her path lay north. She had a mission, a fortune to claim for their two boys, and a gold rush to experience. She

The City of Seattle *carrying the gold rush north. Steamboats, scows, cattle boats, anything that would float, were filled with men, horses, donkeys, goats, sheep, all headed to Skagway or Dyea where trails led over the mountains to the headwaters of the Yukon River. Yukon Archives, H.C. Barley Fonds, 82/298 5138.*

would not turn back, with or without her husband. She wrote Will that she was going north as planned; that he was undependable and she never wanted to see him again.

She never would.

Her next problem was with her brother George, who was refusing to take her without her husband. He came close to sending for Father to come and take her home. Martha pleaded, cried and threatened to go north by herself. She finally convinced George to take her and not tell their father what had happened until they were part way to the Yukon.

Writing her autobiography, Martha found herself unable to remember details of the Seattle scene. It should have been unforgettable—hordes of people arriving daily to swell the crowds already on the docks, clamouring for tickets on any floating raft heading up the Inside Passage; piles of gear being sorted, being loaded; fevered excitement, noise, anticipation. But Martha's mind was in turmoil, her young life in chaos. Like thousands of others in Seattle and San Francisco who were leaving the chaos of their present lives behind, she could only look north for solution and salvation.

They went north on the *Utopia*, which Martha described as a has-been but better than some of the wrecks and tugboats that were heading up the Inside Passage, where fog, wind, rocks and uncharted waters would play havoc with them. At least three ships a month were wrecked on the thousand-mile voyage. Their trip took seven days, and the lengthening daylight as they moved north increased Martha's ability to clear her mind of personal problems and see the majestic scenery around her: the totem poles on the shores, the glaciers and icebergs, orcas and schools of dolphin in the water. After a stop at Skagway, they were deposited at Dyea.

The Tlingit people had a long history of using the trail over the Chilkoot to trade with inland nations. Their control of the Chilkoot Pass gave them power and wealth. The arrival of thousands of white men added to that wealth as they became packers paid to carry heavy loads up the trail. Martha watched them bearing loads twice as heavy as most newcomers could carry.

Now, here she was, at the top of the Chilkoot, which felt like the top of the world, and she must not look back. The bed Colonel Spencer found for her in the Tacoma Hotel was a piece of canvas stretched on four logs, but it afforded her the best sleep she had ever had.

Their whole party rested the next day until evening, then walked the two miles to Lake Bennett, where they hoped to find their gear waiting for them. It had not arrived yet. At Bennett, the wood and canvas hotels had no bed for Martha, although one man offered to share his bunk with her. George arranged with a packer that they could sleep in some canvas-covered hay if they promised not to scatter it about. Here, the six of them slept for several nights, until two Australians offered them a cabin near Lake Lindeman which they were vacating. The Munger party walked back there to camp while waiting for their gear to arrive and waiting for their boat to be built on Lake Bennett.

Martha would remember these two weeks as the best camping experience of her life: the blue lake ringed with snow-capped mountains, the warm sunlight on the cool mountain air. Daytime took over the night as they reached the vernal equinox and the sun lingered until midnight. They were like kids on a campout, the men hunting for blue grouse and ptarmigan that they roasted on an outdoor fire, Martha learning to make sourdough bread and baking pies and doughnuts. Sometimes George managed to gaffe a fish with a forked stick.

For Martha, this was a time to explore the slopes and find mountain forget-me-nots, pink snakeweed, mountain harebell and cerise shooting stars. On lower levels she found Dutchman's breeches, bleeding heart, twin flowers. She watched sun-dew trap unwary insects in its hairy leaves. In parks and fields around Chicago, she had begun a collection of wild flowers, and her knowledge was already extensive. But here she was finding varieties that were new and exciting. Here in the Yukon, wild flowers would become an abiding passion. Sometime during these idyllic two weeks, she felt herself falling in love with this vast and amazing land.

Once, their camp was visited by a bear that helped himself to a ham and a tin of butter. But it was a mouse that ran up her sleeve and out the back of her nightgown that woke the camp, thanks to Martha's shrieks. One tobacco-chewing old-timer liked to tell the story: "Walked over the pass. Goin' through the rapids. Campin' a long way from home. Pretty rough life. Ain't afraid of nuthin' but a mouse. Lordy! Wimmin is queer."[8]

When they walked to Bennett to check on the progress of their boat, there was time to get to know some of the hopes and dreams of the swirling mass of humanity gathered here. There were 10,000 people in this tent town wrapped around Lake Bennett in the spring of '98. Climbers from both the Chilkoot and the White Pass converged here, waiting for the ice to go out. There were saloons, tent hotels, a Presbyterian church in a tent, goods of all sorts to be sold here or carried on to Dawson. The sweet smell of new-sawn lumber mingled with wood smoke. Men swore at each other as they whipsawed lumber to build their boats. It was said that two angels could not whipsaw a log into lumber without getting into a fight. Other men stood in line for hours to pay high prices for each piece of sawn lumber. Martha talked to men who had left their farms, their jobs, their wives and sweethearts, their motherless children to seek their fortune in this place; it seemed to help them to talk to a woman here.

There were doctors, lawyers, dentists and company managers struggling to learn new skills and wondering how they were going to get down the Yukon. Like the Mungers, they were paying skilled carpenters to have their boats built. The Munger boat was being built at King's Shipyard and would cost $275. It would look like a dory, 37 feet long and made of Alaska pine. Captain Spencer oversaw the building and pronounced her river-worthy.

In their new craft, they set out clad in oilskins as heavy rain poured down and a stiff wind blew.

Next morning was clear and bright, and still windy. With blanket sails erected, they sped along into the narrow waters called Windy Arm. Here they were twice forced to land on leeward shores because the wind was too strong.

They moved always in a parade of watercraft. Although thousands had preceded them, pushing off from Bennett in late May, the minute the ice went out, there were thousands more like themselves pushing off in June and July. There were canoes that had been carried over the pass, large scows with oxen or horses, pigs or sheep on board. They saw outriggers, kayaks, shaky rafts and cockleshells. When they reached Lake Tagish and its Mounted Police post, they were counted in as boat number 14,405. Since May, 18,000 men had passed by here. Women were counted separately, and Martha learned she was number 631. Most of the women heading north were dance-hall girls and/or prostitutes; there was the odd wife determined to accompany her husband, and the odd reporter or adventuress.

While all travelers were stopped here, the Mounties searched each boat for alcohol. While this went on, Martha had been urged by the men to make herself comfortable on two boxes that were covered with blankets and furs. Afterward, the men told her she had been sitting on their cases of scotch whisky.

After Marsh Lake, a river poured into Miles Canyon, narrowing abruptly as it squeezed between hundred-foot rock walls, pushing up into four-foot waves, then erupting into rapids that looked like stampeding white horses.

Miles Canyon and the White Horse Rapids would test every craft headed to Dawson. The *avant garde* had plunged recklessly into its maelstrom, and in that first rush 150 boats were swamped and ten

gold-seekers lost their lives. Traffic jammed up as boatmen pondered how to get through alive. If a man did not go through Miles Canyon—if he paid someone to cart his boat around—there would be something missing years later when wanted to brag about his Trail of '98.

Mounties arrived on the scene and stopped fragile rafts, boats without enough freeboard or captains without enough water knowledge. They also decreed that women and children should leave their boats and walk the five miles around the canyon and rapids.

Before the Munger party committed themselves to the canyon, they heard that they risked a hundred-dollar fine if a woman was on board, but Martha could not face the five-mile walk alone. She had faith in Captain Spencer's skill and experience. She insisted on riding through, and the men let her.

The roller-coaster whirlpool in the canyon shot them out into the White Horse Rapids, with its boulders that smashed hulls and its jagged rocks that ripped at bottoms. There was a bad moment when the steering oar broke and the boat swung around. Spencer grabbed another oar and shouted to the men to let the boat go through "stern to." Twenty-six minutes after they entered the canyon, they were out of the rapids into quiet water, and laughing in relief.

When they camped in the little tent city that would become Whitehorse, they had their first all-out attack from Yukon mosquitoes. Badly bitten, they got underway at dawn and vowed to camp on higher land as they started the 380-mile journey down the Yukon River to Dawson.

OPPOSITE: *Miles Canyon and Whitehorse Rapids made an obstacle course of punishing water power, which had to be run by every boat headed to the Klondike goldfields. Yukon Archives, T.R. Lane collection, 82/280 1391.*

There were Mounted Police stationed at Lake Laberge and again at Five Fingers Rapids. At the rapids, they warned boaters to keep to the right bank as they approached the four standing rocks with five fingers of water pushing between. The right-hand path looked dangerous, but the swirling current here would shoot your craft away from the rock and into the clear.

Day by day now, they moved downstream. The swift river talked to them, its sounds incessant. As it swirled and eddied over its uneven bottom, it threw sediment noisily against the sides of the boat, a powerful yet peaceful sound. The air was fragrant from the willows along the shore. They spotted eagles in the trees. There were birds on the high, ragged cliffs that Martha would later learn to call peregrine falcons. A kestrel perched in a dead tree. A family of mergansers were lined up beside a small island. When they stopped for the night, they cooked dinner on their little sheet-iron stove. Sometimes dinner was squirrel, sometimes waterfowl, but more often salmon, whitefish or grayling caught along the way. Often, they could sleep under the stars, wrapped in mosquito nets.

They were always part of the moving flotilla—boats of all kinds, some so crude that only sheer luck could have got them through the Whitehorse Rapids. Martha saw one boat cut in half, evidence of a partnership gone sour.

They were two nights above Dawson when they camped by a small creek and met a party from New Zealand that had staked their claims here. Martha invited them to supper, and in the evening they all sang songs together. They said they were thinking of naming the creek "Maori." Martha suggested *Excelsior*, a word meaning superior and the name of the ship that took the first gold to San Francisco. Everyone liked the name, and the creek became Excelsior. In the morning George and Martha staked their first Yukon claims on Excelsior Creek.

Over the Chilkoot

As they neared Dawson, no one knew how near they were. Other people on the river, like themselves, had never been there. Opinions varied from "just around the corner" to "another hundred miles." They did know it was on the right bank of the Yukon and they hugged that shore in fear of being swept past.

Like every new arrival, they were gob smacked by their first sight of Dawson City. As they rounded the bend where the Klondike River flows into the Yukon, oars were stilled in mid-air as occupants stared. Whatever they had expected, this sprawling city of tents, cabins, shacks, cache structures on stilts, hotels, saloons and churches spread over the flats below a scar-faced dome, surpassed their imagination. Here were 20,000 people in motion, sawing, pounding, toting, recording claims, cooking, washing, bartering, and brawling. Here was their city of gold.

Where to fit in looked like a problem. The only way to land was to tie your boat to another boat, which was tied to another and so on. George soon discovered that building lots were now pushing up against the mountain or into marshland. They were also too expensive for the Mungers' dwindling funds. They crossed the river and settled on a hill above the area called Lousetown, where the ladies-of-the-night lived.

While the men chopped trees and hewed logs for their cabin, Martha wrote home. "Of my children I say nothing, but mean much. I have no fear for them, only an all-abiding faith that all is well. … P.S. Will has gone to the Sandwich Islands. I never want to see him again."[9]

There was not a lot of summer left when their party arrived on August 5. Days shorten rapidly in the Yukon, and already the crowberries and kinnikinnick were turning red on the hills. As the men worked long days to erect a large cabin, Martha set out on her mission to claim the Lambert gold.

She visited the Gold Commissioner's office and asked to see the records and find registration of the Lambert claim. Her considerable charm produced no result until she resorted to bribing the clerk. Then she found the records unreliable, names and dates erased or scratched out, sometimes even cut out. She found no sign of a Lambert staking a claim anywhere.

Next, she tried the post office, hoping to track down the men who had witnessed the Lambert will. These men were real because mail was being held for them. Martha finally paid a post office employee one hundred dollars to open the letters. There was no useful information in them. She watched the smiling employee write "opened by mistake" on the envelopes, her hundred dollars stashed away in his coat pocket.

She tried writing letters to the witnesses but never had a reply. She searched for Lambert's grave but found no sign of it. She did find that a prospector named Lambert had existed and was last heard of in Juneau, Alaska. Someone also said that they recognized his handwriting on the will. But there her trail went cold.

For a time, she kept busy making their log cabin homey. The men had constructed a table with two wide boards and poplar legs. They made willow withy chairs and benches. A packing box made a cupboard. Martha had insisted on bringing a bolt of cretonne printed with "roses on a sage green background," and with this she sewed curtains and covers for cushions that she stuffed with wild duck down. She spread out their furs on the bunks and hung any extra blankets on the log walls. She had oilcloth for the table, and on it she put wild flowers in a tin can that she had wrapped in birchbark. They were six adults playing house and all proud of what they made.

But Martha was not proud of herself. As she watched men sell their gear and push off up the river, she knew these were the ones who had failed to find gold at the end of their rainbow. As she had failed to find hers.

Over the Chilkoot

The beauty of autumn in the Yukon, the low sun highlighting the blue river running smooth past dark spruce trees and red-gold hills, belied the inevitable coming of harsh Yukon winter. But old Sourdoughs knew, and they liked to tell Chechakos (newcomers) the stories of the winter before. Almost 5000 people were in Dawson for the "starving winter" of 1897.

When the steamers had not arrived by September or had arrived with whisky instead of food-stuffs, or diminished loads because men downstream had usurped the supplies, there was desperation in Dawson. The two trading companies, the North American Trading and Transportation and the Alaska Commercial, tried to prevent individuals from hoarding the insufficient supplies; they refused to fill large orders already paid for, causing near-riots. The Mounted Police and the Gold Commissioner walked the streets, urging men to get out while they could.

Some took passage on the steamers, only to be stranded part way down the Yukon as ice jammed and stopped the boats. Others headed upstream, suffering terribly on the passes, only to reach Dyea or Skagway with frozen fingers, toes or limbs that had to be amputated. Now, in the fall of '98, as the stories were told, unease seeped into cabins and tents. Did they have enough? Could 10,000 to 20,000 of them get through this winter?

There were many reasons for leaving. A gold strike in September in Nome, Alaska, lured a number of men. They scrambled to get down the river before freeze-up. They heard the gold was lying in the sand on the beaches, which made it easy picking compared to Klondike digging. Maybe you didn't even need a claim. Other men, lonesome for home, were giving up. On the long days of June and July, you could believe you would strike it rich at any moment. Now your claims were worthless or stolen through fraud in the registry office, your back ached, your stomach growled from a diet of beans, and a dance hall girl had most of your money. You could not make it through the winter. You would have to leave Dawson in the early fall. When ice formed on the river in early October, you knew you had missed the boat.

Martha's unease was becoming panic as she faced her own failure. How could she have been so foolish as to believe that a million dollars in gold dust was just waiting for her to retrieve it? But a fear more immediate than lost gold or possible starvation was assailing her. She was pregnant!

While she decorated the cabin, while she pursued the lost Lambert fortune, she had been able to push this to the back of her mind, but ever since her breakdown at the top of the Chilkoot, she knew. She knew now that she should have found a way to go home. But how? She could not face the Chilkoot Pass alone, and she could not ask George to go. Harry Peachy was talking of leaving with a group of men, but she could not ask them to take her. A railway was being blasted through the rock wilderness north from Skagway, but it would not help her. [It would not reach Bennett until July next year, and it would not reach Whitehorse until 1900.] Now, ice was forming on the river and she was trapped here.

She went secretly to see Father Judge at the Roman Catholic Hospital. She was shocked to hear that hospital and doctor expenses would amount to $1000. She had squandered her funds on a fool's errand. The money advanced by fathers Purdy and Munger that got them to Dawson was running low. Food prices were exorbitant, and there was no payout yet from their claims. She would have to have this baby alone.

As the days darkened, despair and depression overtook her. It was hard not to think of Will enjoying the sun and sand of the Sandwich Islands. Why couldn't she go with him? What was wrong with her?

She was beaten, embarrassed and terrified. There were nights when she prayed to die.

When she told George of her condition, his misery added to her own. He knew he should never have allowed her to come. "Father will never forgive me."

Oddly enough, it was trying to cheer up her brother that got her out of the depths of despair. That and what she called her "old fighting spirit." She'd had two babies before. She could do this. This infant would need clothes. She took stock of the two tablecloths and two dozen napkins she had, and began to sew by candlelight.

By American Thanksgiving, they had been frozen in for five weeks. But Martha's spirits had recovered enough to make mincemeat and plan a celebration dinner for her own five plus three guests. In a letter home, she gives the menu:

>
> Canned Tomato Soup – Bread Sticks
>
> Oyster Patties – Olives
>
> Baked Stuffed Ptarmigan
>
> Canned Corn – Desiccated Potato Puff
>
> Bread – Butter – Pickles
>
> Mince Pie – Cheese – Coffee
>
> Popcorn Balls – and a taste of your Home Fruit Cake
> (the larger part of this to be saved for Christmas). [10]

There was talk of monthly mail service for Dawson, but no one really believed it would happen. Nevertheless, Martha wrote long letters to Warren and Donald, hoping they might reach the boys. She described Dawson and the rivers and valleys in summer and again in winter. She hoped they were not missing her too much. But sometimes she was so lonesome herself that she hoped they were.

On long nights when she could not sleep, her mind took her back to Chicago and the house where she was born and the parents she described as a study in contrasts, her mother the daughter of a Kentucky plantation owner, her father a Yankee who fought in the Civil War. Susan Owens' mother died when she was five and she was sent, along with two sisters, to Germany and France to be educated. She came back in 1864 and was sent to an uncle in Cincinnati. That was where she met George Munger, a Yankee recovering from wounds acquired at the battle of Seven Pines.

The pressure on George to succeed was huge. He was a laborer working for his father in the Pennsylvania oilfields. He was twelve years older than Susan, marrying a very young, cultured, educated Southern girl whose family objected strenuously to the match.

His situation got worse when the oil refinery burned. He and Susan moved to Chicago, where he found work in the linen department of Ross and Gossage. On a Sunday walk one morning, he saw a for-sale sign on a laundry and, with a friend backing him, he was able to buy it. Owning a laundry did nothing to elevate his image in the Owens family.

Those were hard years for Susan Owens Munger, educated in European fine arts. In four years, she bore five children. Three died as infants, one of them Martha's twin. Martha's crippled sister, Agnes, lived until the age of three.

George's laundry prospered. By 1871, he had a new plant and enough money to give Martha a thousand dollars to buy a sealskin jacket and a velvet dress. Along with pleasing his wife, he was broadcasting his success to her intractable family.

That success was short-lived. At 9:25 on October 8, 1871, in O'Leary's barn on the west bank of the Chicago River, fire broke out.

By ten o'clock, the city of Chicago was on fire, people fleeing for their lives.

Fire became Martha's earliest memory! She was five years old. Her father burst into the house yelling that they had to run, that they could save nothing but themselves, that he did not have five hundred dollars for a wagon. Martha's mother calmed him down and reminded him that she still had the thousand dollars he had given her. That money, intended for a fur coat, let George hire a wagon and load it with bedding and foodstuffs, then pack in little lame Agnes, then sick Aunt Edith, Martha and her mother. Men and servants would walk.

Martha's memories of that race to the lakeshore included conveyances of every sort—wheelbarrows, wagons, stretchers, baby carriages. There were black and bloody faces, screaming children, stampeding horses and cattle, rats escaping the flames. Years later she could still feel the heat, hear the terrible roar.

When they reached Lake Michigan, the October wind was cold. Aunt Edith no longer moved, and Martha would understand later that she had died. They slept under the wagon that night. By morning, Chicago was a smoking ruin.

Some 98,000 people lost their homes, and 250 died in the fire. Charity flowed into Chicago and the city began to build small houses on Wapense Avenue for the homeless. The Munger family could move out of a tent into one of the houses.

George Munger was deeply humiliated to be moving his family into an area already dubbed Poverty Flats. There would be no sealskin jacket for Susan now.

What Martha remembered of her mother during those difficult times was that she never complained and never lost faith in "dear Father." On the subject of money, she said that no lady ever talked of money, whether she had it or not.

Martha was more her father's daughter and did not take kindly to being poor. Across from Poverty Flats were substantial houses that had not burned. When Martha tried to play with children there, their mother chased her away, declaring no ragtag-bobtails from Poverty Flats would play with her children. Martha marched home straight and tall and furious, but the shame of that moment stayed with her all her life.

Relatives came to George with financial aid. His father, who now owned a drugstore in Galva, Illinois, arrived as quickly as he could. Help also came from Charles Morse of the Fairbanks-Morse Company, who was married to Susan's sister. The Morse company had begun with a patent on platform scales and expanded to produce steam engines, electrical motors, diesel engines, rail cars and farm machinery. The Morses had just returned from the Paris Exposition, and they brought Martha a Paris doll and a white embroidered dress, which she used to lord it over those well-off children across the street.

Martha had not inherited her mother's equanimity. Once, in a rage she attacked a playmate and left her badly scratched. Martha's mother had been making her a beautiful dress, and as punishment for her behavior she gave it to the little girl Martha had hurt. Martha remained more sorry about the dress than the little girl. Looking back, she described herself as "naturally hot headed and vain" and supposed she had never been cured of those faults.

With the help of his relatives, George was able to re-establish his laundry business. The family moved to a brick house on North Franklin Street. By the time gold was discovered in the Yukon, he had a lucrative laundry business and would be able to help finance a party bent on finding gold.

Meanwhile, he had a rambunctious daughter to educate. He took Martha out of high school and placed her in a "finishing" school for "young ladies." George set the bar high for his children: "Some day one of my girls may be the wife of the President of United States and live in the White House, and I want her to know how to fill a position like that. On the other hand, one of my girls may have to work for the President's wife, and I want her to know how to do that equally well."[11]

But the teachers at the finishing school gave up on Martha, and she was taken out again. Looking for a solution to Martha, Susan Owens remembered her convent education in France. She and George found a school of the same order in Indiana—St. Mary's of Notre Dame.

Although Martha's family was Protestant, her Catholic education shaped her in many ways. The nuns somehow managed to teach her manners, etiquette and deportment. She may not have learned discretion and caution, but she learned grace and dignity, which served her well even when she left the beaten path. As part of the study of deportment, the girls had to curtsy to the portrait of Queen Victoria until they could do it to perfection. In later years, when presented to a Prime Minster or a Governor General or Queen Mary or Queen Marie of Romania, she would know precisely how to act, and she would curtsy perfectly.

Martha would describe her time there as five of the grandest years of her life. She discovered a world of great beauty: the grounds, with paths and gardens along the St. Joseph's River, and more beauty to be found in the study of botany. She also loved elocution—the feeling of power and importance it gave her to recite to the class. She was chosen class poet. When she graduated in 1886, she won the elocution medal and took top honours for her herbarium collection of dried flowers.

There was one bad moment at her graduation, when the girls were given conduct awards—gold for best behaviour, silver for second place, and green for "just get by." Martha received the green. Her spirits sank but rebounded quickly when flowers arrived from admirers. Hers from a young man named Will Purdy were the most exquisite.

Will was a student at the Morgan Park Military Academy. During her school holidays, Martha went home to Chicago, where she was allowed to attend evening parties once she turned 18. At one of these parties, she met Will. When he graduated and started working in the paymaster department of the Chicago and Rock Island Railway, he and Martha were married.

Now in the Yukon, although she tried not to think of Will Purdy, he was there in the shadows of her mind, making up a large part of her humiliation, her failure. He was the father of her little boys, who did not know yet that their father was gone out of their lives.

As the days darkened, their food dwindled and they regretted the largesse of their Thanksgiving dinner. Prices in Dawson reflected the scarcity of supply. For six months, the Munger cabin had no sugar, milk or butter. They ate cornmeal mush, prunes and tasteless desiccated vegetables. Martha craved fresh fruit and vegetables.

Sitting around their Klondike stove on the dark evenings, the men tried to keep her spirits up with stories they had heard in town. In the dark winter in the Dawson saloons, a good story was worth its weight in gold. Men from the Wild West—gunslingers, buffalo hunters, fur traders, Indian-fighters —this was their last frontier. They came here with their past glories, and over whisky in one of the 20 Dawson saloons, they shared and embellished their stories.

There were big names in Dawson. Frank Slavin, the heavyweight champion, was here. Nelly Bly, who had travelled around the world by herself in 1889-90, was here. Flora Shaw, sent by the Times of London, had walked over the Whitepass with as much style as Martha on the Chilkoot. There were also the dance-hall girls, like Limejuice Lil and The Oregon Mare and Diamond Tooth Gertie, who they said really had a diamond embedded between her two front teeth. None of Martha's men admitted to knowing them personally.

The men talked about Big Alec McDonald, who bought a supposedly worthless claim for a sack of flour and a slab of bacon. They said he now needed 39 mules to carry his gold out from the creeks. The poet Captain Jack Crawford, who had been a friend of Buffalo Bill Cody, now sold ice cream in the summer and hay in the winter and gave you a poem as well. Arizona Charlie Meadows, a famed rodeo king, had produced a souvenir newspaper last summer which made him a fortune. Now the talk was of a dance hall and theatre he planned to build in the spring, to be called The Palace Grand.

Martha liked the story of the two Ceechakos (newcomers) asking the men on Bonanza Creek if there was any unstaked ground, a question no miner was likely to answer. What about the mountainside, they asked. Every Sourdough knew gold was heavy and found in creeks, where centuries of flowing water had deposited it. As a joke they told the newcomers: Sure, stake up on the hill.

The two men staked on a "bench" and built a cabin and sunk a shaft. Now the men on the creek felt guilty as they watched them work in vain high above them. Gold did not climb hills. The newcomers did know enough to look for gravel, and after weeks of digging they found it, but no gold. They went down the hill and told the men there was no gold in the gravel.

"Gravel? There couldn't be gravel!" They went up the hill to see, and there was gravel. They told the two men to keep on digging and keep quiet, and they helped them work. Then one day there was gold in the gravel! In some past eon an upheaval had moved hills and valleys around; the men had uncovered an old riverbed and changed the rules about where gold might be found in the Klondike landscape.

One story concerned Martha and the Lambert will. The Lambert family had expected Martha to return in the fall with their gold. When she did not appear, they suspected foul play. Financed by Gillette, of baking-powder fame, they launched their own expedition to Dawson, planning to come in by St. Michael's. A lawyer accompanied a member of the family to St. Michael's, where he was heard boasting about how he would deal with Martha Purdy when he found her in Dawson. But a blond fortune-hunter distracted the young lawyer from his cause and removed him from his money. The men had a good laugh over this one. Martha was just glad that no Lambert party arrived in Dawson to accost her.

There was news about Eli Gage. He and Sophy had reached Eagle, Alaska, in the summer, but there he got sick and the two of them went home. As directed by Captain Spencer, he did sell the boats of the Purdy-Gage company to his father-in-law's Northern Trading and Transportation Company. The Purdy-Gage Company was no more.

There was another story that involved Eli Gage. In the early fall of '97, when all of Dawson was facing starvation and the steamers were stuck downriver on sandbars because the river was so low, one steamer finally got through. It was the N.A.T.T. steamer named the *Portus B. Weare*. Weare's partner, John J. Healey, the old fur trader from Fort Benton, Montana, was stationed at Dawson. Healey ran out of his empty warehouse and up the gangplank to see what food was on board. He found nothing but whisky and hardware, when he had specifically ordered nothing but food and clothing. He was so enraged that he attacked the man that brought it, almost strangling him until onlookers intervened. As the story was told, this was Weare's son Eli. But everyone in the Munger cabin knew that Weare's son, Sophy's brother, was called Will. If the man on board was Eli, then he was Eli Gage, Weare's son-in-law.

Martha with her new baby and her brother, George, in their Dawson cabin. Yukon Archives 82_218_2.

Martha's baby was born on January 31. Martha said he arrived early, but he weighed in at nine pounds, so perhaps not that early. Did Martha leave Seattle knowing she was pregnant? Did she think the Lambert money would get her home by way of St. Michael's in time. Or, did she blunder on in self-denial until it was too late to turn back?

In her biography, she says she was alone for the birth, but years later, talking to Flo Whyard, who edited a later edition of her biography, she said she was helped by two men, an old sea captain and a one-armed man. These would be Captain Spencer and Captain Treat. The two older men were apparently chosen to stay at the cabin until the baby arrived, one man to stay with her, one to go for help if needed.

It was probably good luck that she chose not to have her baby in the Dawson hospital, because typhoid was rampant there that winter. Father Judge tended the sick until he was exhausted and ill. He died of pneumonia just a week before Martha's baby was born. All Dawson mourned the man who had tirelessly given his life to help the sick and homeless in Dawson City.

Martha's baby came easily into the world and seemed happy to be here. Martha named him Lyman, after Grandfather Munger. The men called him The Little Chechako, meaning newcomer or tenderfoot, and he was their hero as they fussed over Martha, kept the fires going, and cooked the meals. Not just their own men but those in the neighbouring cabins were celebrating. They brought ptarmigan, moose, cake and chocolates. Miners and prospectors brought gold nuggets and gold dust as gifts for the baby. They wanted to hold him and talk about their own babies far away. Bath time became a daily show.

On February 10, Martha wrote home. She had not let her parents know a baby was coming. Harry Peachy had managed to get home, but George had warned him not to tell Martha's parents, as they could do nothing to help. Harry kept the secret from Martha's parents but he did tell his own family. He said, "By this time, Martha is dead. She was going to have a baby, and she couldn't possibly live, she looked so ill."[12]

Now Martha sent a curl of Lyman's hair with the news. "Embrace my other little ones for me. Tell them about their new little brother, and be ready to welcome the wanderers."[13]

Here in Dawson, everyone was welcome in the Munger cabin. The little Chechako grew hale and hearty and loved the attention. He was sunshine in the dark winter. As the winter days lengthened and brightened, bit by bit, George and Martha played their mandolin and guitar and the visitors sang old songs and little Lyman gurgled and laughed.

Spring came. Martha and baby were alone in the cabin when thawing snow caused an avalanche of mud and rocks to race down the mountain.

Martha and George can't wait to launch their canoe as the ice leaves the Yukon River. Yukon Archives, 003258.

She grabbed the baby but once outside stood transfixed, not knowing what to do. They were saved by a stand of trees 70 feet above the cabin, which stopped the torrent of snow, mud, rocks, and brush, and split it in two. The heavy right half swept by their cabin, tore up another tree and took out two cabins farther down. The left half came close to Martha, took their outhouses but spared them and the cabin.

On April 26, they watched from their side of the river as fire lit the sky, burning the wood and canvas city of Dawson. More than 100 buildings were lost. Next day, men were sorting through the ashes for the gold dust that sparkled there. Martha's men came home with the story that, during an argument, two dance hall girls in the Bodega Hotel knocked over a lighted lamp, which started the fire. Undaunted,

Dawson quickly rose again, this time with more substantial buildings, and eventually plank sidewalks and a sewer system.

On May 17 in the afternoon, the ice went out of the river. Martha was alerted by a tremendous barking of dogs. Huge blocks of ice were swirling as they sped past Dawson, and on one sat a bobcat, making the huskies go berserk as they ran along the shore after it. Along with the dogs, Martha saw that all the inhabitants of Dawson had rushed to the waterfront in celebration. Watching the power of spring break up the Yukon ice, she experienced a surge of elation. She was now a Sourdough. A Sourdough had at first meant someone who had been here before the 1897 strike, but it had come to mean anyone who had survived a Yukon winter.

Steamers appeared on the river, and thirty sacks of mail arrived, some letters mailed almost a year ago. There was no letter from Will.

On long June evenings, the men were happy to look after Lyman so Martha could search for wildflowers, soaking in the warm evening sun, feeling light and free and rejoicing in every flower find. She found herself remembering Lake Bennett a year ago and comparing its flora with what she was finding here on the mountainsides, the benches and natural pastures. There were blue bells, pyrola, Arctic poppies, Jacob's ladder. Often, she would leave the sandy hills for the boggy places, always on the hunt for orchids. The white orchis, with its pink and purple spots, was abundant. She found the Siberian or Franklin lady-slipper first noted by botanist John Richardson on the Franklin expedition. Then, to her joy she found a rare clump of three pure white orchids.

In July of '99, the White Pass and Yukon Railway reached Lake Bennett from Skagway. One of its first passengers was George Merrick Munger Sr. When mail had finally reached the Mungers in Kansas and they heard the shocking news of Martha's baby, George took the

Dawson City today, seen from the Dome (a towering hill scarred by a landslide). The Klondike River flows into the Yukon from the east. 2.6 mi (4km) upstream is Bonanza Creek where gold nuggets found in the gravel set off North America's greatest gold rush. Photo: Enid Mallory.

first boat north. Martha and her brother, George, could hardly believe their eyes when their father walked into the cabin and soon had little Lyman in his arms. It was a joyous time, and Martha was determined to make her meager food stores into a celebration meal. Her brother went off to Dawson and brought back moose liver and bacon, but he could only procure one huge potato and one medium onion. Dessert was brown bread without butter, rice with molasses, and tea without sugar.

George Munger wanted to take his daughter home at once. What he saw here was a crude cabin and scarcely enough food to eat. When he asked if she had heard from Will and she told him no, nor did she want to, he invited her to live with them at Catalpa Knob.

Martha told him of her claim on Excelsior Creek, how it might make a new life possible for her here. Two strong wills—father and daughter—bandied their arguments back and forth and finally reached a compromise. Martha would go out, leaving her claims in her brother's care. If they did not pay out ten thousand by next summer, Martha would not mention Klondike again.

It was hard for Martha to go. She would see her boys again, and that was wonderful. But it was mid-summer in the Yukon—long hours of sunlight erasing most of the night, rampant green growth, birds singing, the swishing of the blue river with flowers on its banks, the mountains with snow on their tops, this great big land around her. She might never see this again.

1904-1916
Dawson High Society

IN THE SUMMER of '99, the river was alive with watercraft of every kind, including several steamers carrying mail and much-needed food in to Dawson, carrying out passengers and gold dust. Martha and her father left on the *Canadian*, which was heavily loaded with people and gold. As the boat pulled away from Dawson, Martha was leaving as a Sourdough. She had seen summer turn to winter and back again. She had seen the flowering exuberance of a Yukon summer, but she had also watched the northern lights in winter. She had stood outside when the hillside below their cabin was enveloped in the white mist that occurs at 50 below. She had seen the iridescent lights play through the mist in green and gold otherworldly beauty. She had watched the moon join the light show, making the landscape a polished shimmering white while the colour show above danced in the heavens. If she never came back, she must never forget this.

Martha and her father talked to the captain and learned about the boat they were on. The *Canadian* had been built in Victoria, British Columbia. A riverboat, 146 feet long with a 33-foot beam, it had to brave the open Pacific to get to St. Michael's and work its way up the Yukon to Dawson, arriving in 1898. Now, in '99, when they reached

Five Fingers Rapids the little steamer almost came to grief. A whirlpool forced her against a finger of rock and smashed part of her upper deck. Passengers stopped breathing, but a skillful crew got her out of there, still afloat.

At Whitehorse there was now a tram to get them around the rapids and the canyon. Then a river steamer took them to Bennett and the new railroad, which would carry them to Skagway in only two hours. Beginning in May of 1898, construction crews totaling 35,000 men worked in the mosquitoes and rains of summer and the extreme cold of an Alaska-Yukon winter to build this mountain railway in a little over a year. They used 450 tons of explosives to blast a right-of-way through the solid rock of the White Pass. They tunneled through the mountain, spanned chasms, worked on cliff edges, carved switchbacks. They got the job done, and the first train headed up the mountain on July 6, 1899.

From the train, the scenery was magnificent, the sun shining on snow-capped mountains, tumbling waterfalls and glaciers that sparkled like blue-green jewels. But superimposed on all that beauty, Martha sometimes saw the struggling men of the year before, frozen, exhausted, panicked; and the horses beaten, screaming as they fell off the cliffs.

Wherever she went, Martha also saw the flowers, even from the White Pass train. Where they crossed streams, she looked down on marsh marigolds, and in other places, goldenrod. Vegetation became more lush as they approached the coast—columbines, sumach, sedges, raspberry and currant bushes and, on the edge of Skagway, abundant chocolate lilies.

|| OPPOSITE: *The White Pass Railway was pushed up and over the mountain from Skagway by a crew of men working in bone-cracking cold and cruel winds in the winter of 1899. Photo: Gord Mallory.*

In Skagway and on the ship to Vancouver, she experienced the exhilaration of mingling with people and ordering whatever she wanted to eat, after being shut in all winter and counting every mouthful of food so she would not run out. When they reached home, her boys were jumping up and down to see her; her 16-year-old sister, Belle, was anxious to get to know her older sister.

In her autobiography, she wrote, "The ranch was a gorgeous spectacle of beauty and plenty."[14] There were the sounds of life everywhere: hens cackling, roosters crowing, turkeys gobbling. Birds sang in the mulberry trees. Bees buzzed, and butterflies flitted over the flower beds that surrounded the mansion her father had built ten years ago. In 1888, he had moved his family to the Catalpa Knob ranch, shortly after Martha had married Will and was living at Walden near Chicago.

When George bought the 1600-acre ranch in 1885, his laundry empire had already made him rich. His invention of the first mechanized steam-laundry machine was paying him handsome royalties. The man who made his fortune in city laundries now wanted to spend it creating his own Garden of Eden.

The rocky and dry soil of the high prairie would need water to grow George's dream. He put his mechanical genius to work creating an elaborate steam-powered system of irrigation, using water from a 90-acre lake which he had made by damming a stream on the property. He planted 130 acres of apples and pears and 160 acres of catalpa trees. Catalpas grew quickly and could be harvested for fence posts and telegraph poles. Vegetable farmers rented irrigated land from him, and a circus wintered its animals on the ranch. Martha saw fields of golden grain, fruit ripening on trees, grape arbours, mulberry trees, gardens lush with vegetables, healthy dairy cows, beef cattle, pigs and horses.

Her father loved nature in all its dimensions. He would wake her up at dawn to watch birds with him. He was known now as the Johnny

Appleseed of the day, or The-Man-Who-Planted-Trees. The state governor appointed him regent of the Kansas State Agricultural College. His mansion was known for hospitality and lively entertaining.

In the long run, his grand experiment would not be a financial success and the ranch would sometimes be referred to as "Munger's Folly." But it was an intrinsic success because he had turned arid land into a reforested and flowering paradise, where wildlife and domestic animals thrived and birds flocked to nest. He showed others what could be done with irrigation. And he was never happier. No wonder he had wanted to remove Martha from her rough cabin and bare cupboard and bring her home to his proud abundance at Catalpa Knob.

Catapla Knob was so beautiful, her parents were so kind, so glad to have her home, so accepting of her wayward ways, she should be happy here, she kept telling herself.

Winter came, with dust storms at first, then blizzards. Martha's spirits sank. Her belief in herself crumbled. She had failed in her marriage and failed in her Klondike mission. Her children were happy here, almost as if they didn't need her. She was 33 years old, and she could see not see any road ahead for herself.

The Martha who loved beautiful things, especially beautiful clothes, now did not care what she wore or how her hair looked. The abundant food that seemed so delicious when she arrived no longer tempted her. Her weight dropped to 90 pounds. The days dragged on.

One day, she overheard her distraught parents talking, her mother saying, "George, what can we do for Martha? We have lost our beautiful daughter."[15]

Her ingratitude suddenly overwhelmed her. Her parents had done so much for her. She saw herself in a mirror—old-looking, glum-faced, her hair in an old-woman knot. She fixed her hair and found a better

|| *Thirty to forty thousand people walked the streets of Dawson in 1899, N.A.C. C6648.*

dress. At dinner, she asked her father if he would buy her some new clothes.

"Anything you want, daughter." Off they went to Chicago on a shopping spree. While there, they visited Father Purdy, who was still hoping she and Will might resume their life together. Martha made it clear that this could not happen. In that case, Father Purdy said, he wanted to help with the education of his son's children. Martha's mind was not settled enough yet to make a decision like that, but she thanked him and kept his offer open.

Back at Catapla Knob, she asked herself what she could do for herself and her boys. When she dared to look at her future, she saw not the Kansas early spring but the Yukon snow and "its mysterious drawing power." She could shut her eyes and see the dark winter skies, with their flashing, pulsing northern lights; she could see the river in spring, exuberant with melting snow, the blue lakes of summer, and autumn hills carpeted with mosses and bright berries.

She had one small thread of hope; she tied her dreams to her placer diggings on the little creek she had named Excelsior. "What I wanted was not shelter and safety, but liberty and opportunity." In June, the long-awaited letter from George arrived. There was gold! Her claim was paying off. She was going back!

She had the blessing of both parents as she packed up to go. Her father was now caught up in the Klondike excitement and was making plans to bring his son and daughter mining equipment next summer. He would bring the family as well. In the meantime, she would need to leave her baby behind, along with eight-year-old Donald. She would have to find work in Dawson, and she could not do this with two small children. But 11-year-old Warren would come with her.

Back in the Yukon, Martha used money coming in from Excelsior to form a partnership with two men to work their claims at Gold Hill, where the Bonanza and Eldorado creeks met, an area that had already made some men very rich. They built a cabin, a storehouse and a bunkhouse for a 16-man operation. The miners had grueling work. They build fires to thaw the ground, then shoveled earth into wheelbarrows, then into sluice boxes. They dug ditches or built flumes to get water down the hillsides to their work site. Water and a rocking motion would make the gold settle to the riffles in the bottom of the box, while the water washed the sand and gravel away. Some outfits were beginning to replace the bonfires with steam pipes and pumps powered by boilers. On their claim, Martha was cook, cleaning lady and washer-woman, along with looking after Warren. It was not an easy life, but she was free, she was in the Yukon, and she was supporting herself.

By the time Martha's family arrived in the summer of 1901, her prospects at Gold Hill had dimmed, and her father set her up in a mill instead. He had brought in a sawmill, a Tremaine Prospecting Mill and a hydraulic monitor. The monitor was a device for directing a high-pressure jet of water to wash away earth and rocks, using a swizzle nozzle attached to a metal rod or "point" pounded into the earth. The hydraulic monitor was installed at Excelsior, where George was in charge. The mills were positioned on the bank of the Klondike, a mile up from Dawson, and Martha's father lost no time building a six-room cabin they named Mill Lodge, an assay office and small cabins for workers.

For Martha, this was a special time, with all her family here, the older boys helping with the work and learning about construction and having fun together, and little Lyman entertaining them all with his antics. This was now Martha's home and her chance for independence. She would be manager of both a sawmill and a quartz mill.

When her parents went home, they took Warren. It had been a hard and sometimes lonely winter for a 12-year-old on Gold Hill. Warren needed schooling, and Martha made the decision to accept Father Purdy's offer to look after Warren and his education. His grandfather would put him into Notre Dame High School in the fall. She said goodbye to her oldest son, already wondering if she was making a mistake. Donald and Lyman would stay with her.

Before they left, they had news that President McKinley had been shot on September 6 at the Pan-American Exposition in Buffalo. He died on September 14. This brought back memories of the day Chicago's mayor was shot at the end of the Columbian Exposition. The Chicago paper that Martha's father received carried an interview with Eli Gage, who said his father could neither eat nor sleep. Lyman Gage had lost a personal friend as well as a President.

For a time, everything went well at Martha's mill. The wife of her watchman agreed to work as her housekeeper and help look after Lyman. When spring came, work accelerated. Martha's day started at seven and sometimes lasted until two or three in the morning. Logs coming in from upriver had to be checked and she had to see to the scaling of lumber going out. She had two crews to supervise. She had had to fire her salesman because he was always drunk, so now she had taken on the business of selling as well. She was often exhausted. Her foreman, Brockman, had control of the men and got the work done, but he was a prickly character who resented Martha and grumbled about being "run by a skirt."

Martha was walking a tightrope, because she needed these men to get the spring work done. It was a seemingly small matter that resulted in a crisis. She asked Brockman to see that the men put their tools away at the end of a shift—peavies, wrenches, wheelbarrows. Expecting cooperation, she got anger instead. "You rich folks is always grochin' and pinchy. Ain't you got a whole storehouse full of tools?"[16]

Her family gone home, her brother 100 miles [165 km] away at the Excelsior site, she had only a housekeeper and two little boys for support. She turned to eight-year-old Donald for help. Each night, he would make sure all the tools were put away.

One morning she found a hammer, an oil can and a wrench lying on the wet path. There was a wheelbarrow dumped in the brush. When she questioned Donald, he said he always put everything away but now he had to put lots of tools away twice. Someone was doing this on purpose.

She accosted Brockman, who swore at her, said he'd had enough of being ordered about by a damn skirt, and quit.

Martha said, "Fine," and went to make up his wages. She looked up to see the whole crew facing her. Brockman said she could take back what she'd said or the whole crew would quit, and that would shut down her "little old tin-pot mill." Martha told him to take his cheque and get out.

All of the men stood with Brockman, except for a likeable young man named Ed, and he had written on a shingle that she should send his pay with his friend Jack.

She asked Donald to accompany the men to the mill to get their belongings while she made up their cheques. Then, shaking with hurt and anger and close to tears, she watched her men walk away.

Donald sidled up to her and said, "Never mind, Mother, I'll work for you."[17]

She and her eight-year-old went out to shut down the machinery in the mill and bank the fires. Suddenly Sergeant Smith of the Mounted Police was there, wanting to know what was wrong. Ed had gone straight to the barracks to tell the police there was trouble at Martha's mill.

The Mountie insisted on leaving a man at the mill while she went over the cantilever bridge to Dawson to rustle up another gang. She found that Brockman was telling everyone not to work for her, but there were plenty of men in Dawson who had failed to strike it rich and they all needed work. She soon had a complete crew.

That night about two o'clock, as the last load of sluice-box lumber was leaving the yard, she and a very tired boy were eating sandwiches by the window in Mill Lodge when they saw a hunched-over figure enter the mill. They ran out but could not find anyone. In their weariness they decided that a workman had come back for something he had forgotten that morning.

Her new foreman, Dandy Smith, had his crew ready to start in three days. When they set the machinery in motion, they were assailed by a screeching noise. The men raced to shut the engine down and then found the bearings and oil cups had been filled with steel filings. Their quick response saved her machinery.

While the men cleaned and repaired, Martha phoned the police. She told them of the furtive figure seen in the night. The police questioned the men who had worked for her and only Brockman lacked an alibi, but she could not prove his guilt. Brockman continued to boast about "getting her" until the police had heard enough to order him out of the country. In Dawson, when the Mounties told you to go upriver, you went.

He left by boat, shouting back that he would "get that hell cat yet." Martha claimed in her biography that she was not afraid, that she had faith in the Mounties to protect Dawson citizens, but she probably slept with her gun near at hand.

Sometimes Martha's autobiography does not tell the whole story. Years later, when Francis Parkinson Keyes was writing about her, Martha told her diary: "The strange, sad history of me life … it is a weird one and would be more so if the half could be told."[18] Such remarks make one read between the lines of the sawmill incident. Was Martha so exhausted and stressed that she was difficult to work for? This sawmill was all-important to her. Her marriage had failed, she had failed to find the Lambert fortune, her Gold Hill mine had been a dud. She was working incredibly hard here and expecting the same from her crew. Did all the men leave because they had grievances with her? Or because they feared Brockman?

The other question is why Brockman hated her so much. Most Yukon men seemed to adore Martha. In her biography she mentions having received a marriage proposal every other week. (She suggests that the abundance of men and scarcity of women had something to do with this.) Did Brockman expect more of Martha than a working relationship? Did it occur to him that he might gain an attractive woman as well as her profitable mill? If he was indeed rebuffed by "the skirt," as he called her, this might explain the vitriol in his remarks.

She later learned that Brockman reached American soil only to be arrested for some earlier misdemeanor. Fortunately, he and Martha never crossed paths again.

A year later, there was another incident at the sawmill. One of her workers was buying goods for himself and charging them to her. This time, she decided to hire professional help. A new lawyer named George Black was recommended to her. She found him helpful, knowledgeable and attractive. Within two weeks he had asked her to marry him.

George Black, born in New Brunswick to well-to-do parents, had been called to the bar in 1896. When news of the Klondike strike reached New Brunswick, he gave up his law practice and headed west. He and his party of four left Vancouver in March of '98 with eight horses and sleds and chose the White Pass route. In an interview for the *Toronto Star Weekly* in 1955, he makes no mention of the suffering of man and beast on that trail but says his party got their horses up to the Summit and across the 15 miles to Log Cabin.

Here the Black party sold all but one of their horses and then pushed on to Lake Tagish, where they cut trees and whipsawed lumber to build a scow and lapstreak boat. They fitted it out with a wood-burning pipe boiler and a propeller brought from Fredericton, New Brunswick, and carted over the White Pass. Then they were off to face Miles Canyon. On the Yukon River, their party split up, George's half deciding not to go to Dawson but to try the Hootalinqua River, which flowed into the Yukon north of Lake Laberge. There, on a small creek that they named Livingstone, they staked their claims.

George, with his partner, worked a rich claim there for three years until a flood tore through their diggings and destroyed their operation.

No longer rich, he cut wood for the riverboats and in 1901 made his way to Dawson as a deck-hand on a river steamer.

In Dawson, he presented his barrister's credentials and was admitted to the Yukon bar. For a time, he joined the practice of his uncle John Black. The owner of the steamboat that brought him to Dawson had no money to pay the captain and crew. As a Maritimer, George was familiar with Admiralty Law and knew a seaman's rights. He organized the crew to sue in Admiralty Court. The sheriff had to sell the cargo and the boat, under Seaman's Lien Law, and pay the crew. George had found a niche for his start-up law practice. There were too many steamers on the Yukon in 1901 and not enough freight and passengers; this was not the only boat owner unable to pay his crew. Before long, he also became known as the best criminal lawyer in Dawson.

Martha's first experience with marriage had left her afraid of making a second mistake. It took her two years to marry George Black. Also, there was the fact that she was still married to Will Purdy, and divorce was not acceptable in the society she knew in Chicago. But in 1903, she filed for divorce.

Meanwhile, George Black was very much a part of her life. Both of them loved to be out-of-doors, and they bonded over campfires when they went on hunting trips or explored the hills, while George took photos and Martha found flowers. They were both serious about learning the habits and haunts of birds and animals.

Still today, the Yukon in spring is one of Canada's special places to observe wildlife. Migration routes channel thousands of tundra-nesting birds up the Yukon valley in May. Martha would often get out of bed before daybreak to catch the cacophony of the endless flocks passing over: the honking of Canada geese so uplifting after a long winter; the loud, trumpeting calls of the sandhill or whooping cranes. As a band of light appeared in the east, she could see flock after flock of swans, plovers, sandpipers, mergansers, shovelers, harlequins, oldsquaws [long-tailed ducks] black surf scooters, goldeneyes.

Some of the migrants stopped along the Yukon as ice melted at the edges; others settled on marshy lakes. Martha and George and the boys tramped on snowshoes or launched a canoe when the ice went out. George taught Martha's fatherless boys to shoot and fish, to handle a canoe and build a fire or a wicki-up shelter when it rained. Before long, both boys were asking her to hurry up and marry Mr. Black.

Martha's divorce became final in June 1904. She would have custody of all three boys. On their shared outings, Martha had learned how much she and George Black had in common. She knew he was well-respected in Dawson and as addicted to the Yukon as she was. They were married on the first of August 1904. George's parents made the trip from New Brunswick to attend. His Uncle George Black and a brother, Charles, were also there. Martha does not mention her brother, George, so it is likely he had left the Yukon by now. George, who had always felt responsible for the sister he brought north against his better judgment, could leave knowing that another George would keep an eye on Martha now. Martha had a few friends but no family attending except her two youngest boys. Five-year-old Lyman, who had never seen his biological father, lost no time calling himself Lyman Black.

George was becoming deeply involved in the politics of the Yukon. Martha, the American, knew nothing about Canadian politics but soon learned a lot from George about corruption in Yukon politics. In 1896, after eighteen years of Conservative government, the Liberals had come into power in 1896 just in time to take full advantage of the gold rush, a golden opportunity for rewarding party supporters, no questions asked.

In 1898 an act of Parliament created the Yukon Territory, a vast land of 200,000 square miles.

The territory now had a commissioner (comparable to a Lieutenant Governor) and a council of 10 that would include the Gold Commissioner, Senior Judge of the Territorial Court, Registrar of Land Titles, Comptroller and Commanding Officer of the North West Mounted Police.

In 1902, the territory chose its first Member of Parliament in a blatantly corrupt federal election. A large number of foreigners— Americans, Swedes, Austrians, Australians—were allowed to vote. Ballot boxes from areas that had fewer than 40 eligible voters were returned stuffed full of ballots.

Meanwhile, honest miners encountered greed and fraud in the recording office. They stood in line for days to register their claim, only to be told it was already staked. Records were falsified. Liberal Party supporters somehow acquired big tracts of mining land.

Yukon mining was based on the free-entry system: a man could enter Crown land and stake out a portion of land, then apply to the government for exploration and development rights. Civil servants could not stake or own claims, but mining recorders were in a good position to "cook the books," and in the heyday of Yukon mining, they did. For a sizable bribe, a recorder would change the name on your application to that of the man who paid him the bribe.

A lot of business went on in the back room of the recorder's office, and the average man could not get in there. Instead, he stood in line for hours. James McRae, a miner from Guelph, Ontario, who kept a diary from 1898 to 1901, wrote:

> *I went down to the Department of Corruption this morning and stood in line till nearly one o'clock but I could not get in. The office closes at one o'clock on Saturday to give the lads a chance to divide*

the spoils so they can go to church on Sunday and pray for strength to help them rob the public during the following week.[19]

George and Martha both owned mining claims and had seen firsthand the corruption that went on. George also had considerable experience in defending miners who had had their claims "jumped," or stolen. Martha had had a good look at the falsifying of records as she searched for the Lambert fortune. She would never know if that fortune had really existed before some unscrupulous civil servant found a way to steal it and destroy the evidence.

In the year of their marriage, a territorial election opened Martha's eyes to what was going on, as George threw himself into the campaign, supporting Dr. Alfred Thompson against the entrenched Liberals. The streets of Dawson erupted in violence after a Liberal plot was exposed. Voter lists were to be posted before election day; then the names of known Conservatives would be stroked off to give the Liberals a win.

Citizens went to see the senior judge who had appointed the enumerators. By the time the returning officer was located, an angry mob was waiting for him. The man was grabbed and a rope was put around his neck. Cooler citizens intervened to save him. Terrified enumerators ran to the Mounted Police barracks for protection. A police officer was stationed in front of the senior judge's residence until the election was over. The Liberals were defeated. In the following year, George was elected to the Yukon Council.

1904 had been a dramatic introduction to Yukon politics, but Martha soon found her role, attending meetings with George and entertaining Conservative supporters in their home. She declared that a marriage required, "complete harmony in religion, in country, and in politics,"[20] a surprising point of view for the woman who marched off to the gold fields while her husband, Will, went to Hawaii. So Martha, the American, became a Canadian and an Anglican and a lifelong Conservative.

In the fall, she and George moved to a house in Dawson. In spite of long days and labour troubles, she had been happy at Millhouse. She loved the challenge and liked being part of the Dawson business community. The mill made money and gave her independence. Her Excelsior mining claim had also paid out well, but like so many in Dawson who should have taken the money and run, she grubstaked other ventures and lost it. In her autobiography, she says she will spare readers (and herself, no doubt) the painful details.

Laura Berton, in her book, *I Married the Klondike*, says Martha was shunned at first when she married George Black. She was the woman whose husband had deserted her, who had cooked in a gold camp, who ran a sawmill, who had lived on the hill above Lousetown. Never mind; she would hold her head high. She would be the little girl in the white dress with the doll from Paris. When she began to entertain in her new house, everyone wanted to attend, even the gossips—*especially* the gossips.

While the outside world still pictured Dawson as a raw frontier town, it had become a sparkling little city with a grand sense of itself. Madame Aubert brought in the latest fashions from cities like Paris and New York. She had a solid base market for her gowns in the three layers of Dawson women as analyzed by Martha: the prostitutes; the dance hall girls; the wives of the miners and the odd single woman. Money—or gold dust—was abundant, and the women of Dawson were happy to pay $500 or more for a Madame Aubert gown. For less formal clothes, Martha depended on White's in Woodstock, Ontario, which supplied her with made-to-order garments that always fit and suited her well.

Martha's wedding gown in 1904 was made by Redfern, New York. It was of pearl-grey velvet, with a floor-length skirt lined in blush-pink silk. A 16-inch yoke had rows of shirring and fell into a short train. The high-necked bodice had a lace yoke over blush-pink piping. She carried a muff of pink roses with long pink ribbons, and among the roses were three small birds, one white, one pink, one lemon. Her merry widow hat made of pink roses was tilted to the side, and three more small birds peeked out from it.

There were many occasions to show off your Paris gown, as every holiday on the calendar was celebrated with a ball, beginning with a big one on New Year's Eve. It was an elaborate costume affair. On the following day, women stayed home to receive the men who came calling, in the Scottish tradition of first-footing.

Washington's Birthday Ball followed soon after for all the Americans in Dawson, then the Easter Ball. July 1st and July 4th were big party days. In Dawson, a large population of Americans celebrated with Canadians, sometimes joining the two days and celebrating for four or five days and nights, with parades by day and balls at night. A St. Andrew's Ball would be held in November.

The big event for showing off the Paris gowns was the annual ball in the A.B. Hall. The Arctic Brotherhood was formed by men who had been "inside the watershed prior to the first day of July 1897." With wealth from the mines, they built a large white building in the middle of town. It had a large dance floor with gallery boxes above it and a stage at the front. The Arctic Brotherhood held their inaugural ball on November 20, 1901. It was such a success that a ball was held every two weeks that winter to pay for the hall. As a yearly affair, the A.B. Ball was the big event of the year, a grand and colourful occasion. Mounted Police in their red uniforms, women whirling in their latest gowns and Sourdoughs in tuxedos. The orchestra was superb and illustrates the level of culture to be found in this remote town. Herr Freimuth, violinist and conductor, was a graduate of the Conservatory of Leipzig. Signor Lopez, cornet soloist, had performed at the Royal Opera House in Madrid. Telgmann had been first clarinet in the Boston Symphony Orchestra.

Depending on the year, the black-suited men swirling the colourful ladies might include figures like William Ogilvie, who surveyed the Dawson townsite and was Commissioner of the Yukon from 1898 to 1901; Joe Boyle who changed Yukon mining when he brought in big dredges; Clemmie Burns, secretary to the commissioner; "Duff" Pattullo, chief clerk in the Gold Commissioner's office and later premier of British Columbia. There would be several Blacks, since George had an uncle in town and sometimes a brother. There would also be old-timers like Dick Lowe, veteran prospector and mule-skinner, who staked a fraction on Bonanza Creek that paid out half a million in gold, or Big Alex McDonald, said to own 50 claims, all rich, or Pete McDonald, also rich because he owned the Phoenix Saloon.

When not dancing in the A.B. Hall, young people had tennis in summer, skating parties in winter and ice carnivals with elaborate costumes, card parties for euchre and 500 and whist bridge, which was new. There were all-night poker games for the men.

"At homes" were essential to a woman's social status in Dawson. Once a month, you sent out invitations and held a "day." You served tea, salted almonds, olives, homemade sherbet and homemade fudge. Each of the people you invited would invite you back, so you might need to attend a "day" almost every day of the week. When you were invited to dinner, it was likely to be an eight-course meal complete with place cards, fine china and fine wine.

Life in Dawson let you dance at a ball one night and camp in pristine wilderness the next. As soon as the ice was out of the river, the Black

A shared love of the land took Martha and George canoeing and hiking and camping. Yukon Archives, 003259.

family pushed off in canvas canoes. They pitched their tent on the shore of a river or creek but often slept in the open, in sleeping bags on a bed of boughs covered with their fur rugs. By day, they would launch canoes exploring one way, then the other, and fishing and hunting. For supper, they would cook the fish or wild fowl they caught, or sometimes even big game.

Martha sat on a rock, watching Donald and Lyman building a proper fire, and thought how strong and resilient they were growing, and how knowledgeable with the outdoor skills George was teaching them. At such times her thoughts wandered to Warren. He had finished at Notre Dame, and Father Purdy was entering him in the Naval Academy at Annapolis, Maryland, in the fall. She wondered what his training there would be and wished he could have had more Yukon training in advance.

Dawson High Society

Ptarmigan, both willow and rock were manna from heaven to early miners. Easy to catch, they filled many a cooking pot, a welcome change from bacon and beans. Photo: Enid Mallory.

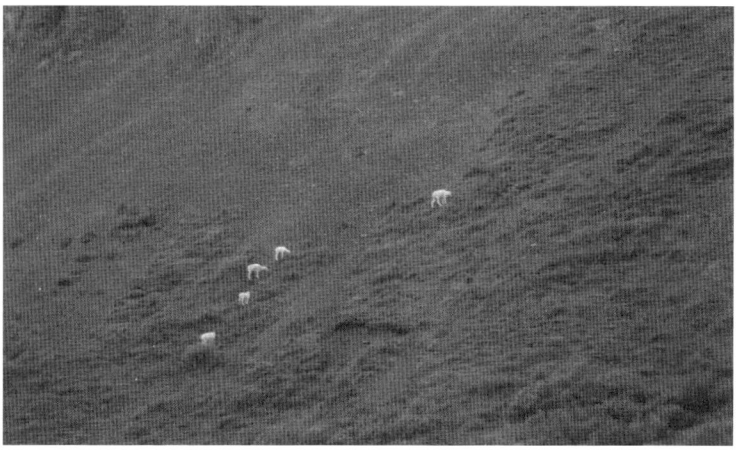

Dawson people hunted moose and bear and caribou when their migration crossed the Yukon River. Big-game hunters climbed the mountains for bighorn sheep and goats. Photo: Enid Mallory.

Martha describes hunting trips where she watched from a blind as the sky lightened in the east and colours changed from grey to silver, then rose and turquoise and crimson, while the sounds of incoming ducks grew louder.

The Black family studied the birds and their habits and habitats and were always on the lookout for unusual birds. When she and the boys spotted a pair of ducks they had never seen before, they worked out a family ambush. The boys carried a canoe upriver to direct the birds downstream while Martha hid in the bushes to signal George. George shot both birds and took the pair of king eider ducks home to perform his taxidermy magic. The two specimens were given to the Canadian Museum in Ottawa.

Martha claimed that the ducks they shot, if not rare like the eiders, were eaten by themselves or their friends. After long, hard winters with limited food choices, a duck or a grouse was a welcome change of diet. They had three varieties of grouse: the beautiful ruffed grouse, the spruce grouse, which old-timers called the "fool hen," and the blue grouse, named for its grey-blue plumage and found on wooded mountains. The sharp-tail grouse was seen only rarely in the Yukon.

The most iconic bird of the Yukon, winter or summer, was the ptarmigan, sometimes called "chicken" by those who could not pronounce or spell the name. They watched the willow ptarmigan turn from mottled brown and white to all-white except for black edges on its tails and wings. Ptarmigan that frequented the higher elevations would turn all-white. These birds, which Martha called rock ptarmigan, are actually white-tailed ptarmigan. The rock, whose range is between the two, have black tips, like the willow. All three varieties nest on the ground and depend on their summer camouflage for survival. Even so, thousands of hungry miners found them to be an easily caught bird for the cooking pot.

Dawson High Society

In the early years both George and Martha were avid hunters. Later they became concerned with conservation and George carried a camera instead of a gun. Yukon Archives, 003253.

Martha fishing from a friend's boat on a Yukon lake. University of Waterloo Archives, WA 19-6-4.

The Blacks also got to know the birds of prey: bald and golden eagles soaring in the sky, goshawks and gyrfalcons, and many of the owls: snowy, great grey, northern, spotted, saw-whet and pigmy. They watched in dismay as gulls swooped down and destroyed duck eggs and ducklings.

Their biggest outdoor thrill was the caribou migration. As the great herds moved south in the fall, their route brought them near Dawson. For days in a row, you could watch them cross the Sixty Mile River. Watching from a distance through binoculars, you had the impression that the earth itself was moving. After this annual event, there were caribou steaks on the tables in Dawson and in the road houses on the Yukon River.

Moose hunters would find a moose-lick (a place where moose were finding much-needed salt); there they would build a blind in a tree and wait in the early morning. Martha often cooked moose-meat but preferred the meat of mountain sheep. Hunting these required a rigorous expedition to alpine heights. Along with other Yukoners, she decried the senseless slaughter of big game by hunters who wanted only trophies while the meat was left to wolves.

Martha said they learned by closely observing wild creatures and birds. Roger Tory Peterson's guide books would not appear until the 1930s. In 1905, Chester A. Reed published the first American bird identification book, called *Bird Guide: Land Birds East of the Rockies*. Chester's "pocket guide" measured three by five inches, which made it perfect for carrying with you on a wilderness trek. By 1906, it had sold 27,000 copies and would begin to let bird watchers identify the bird in the wild without shooting it and taking it home for study. It is possible the Blacks had one of these.

When at home, Martha's doors were always open. The response to her new baby in January of '99 had warmed her heart and taught her about Yukon hospitality. It made her forever mindful of the men who were lonesome for home and wives and sweethearts. Many still missed their mother's cooking; if she had ptarmigan in the pot, she shared with whoever came by.

On election nights she prepared for two to four hundred visitors. She cooked ham and chickens and turkey to make sandwiches stout enough for a Sourdough miner. She made gallons of salads, dozens of cakes, and a lot of punch, both "wet" and "dry." She prepared for a night of wild excitement. No Dawson election was ever mild, she said.

Martha by this time was out of touch with her old Chicago friends, but relatives kept her informed and often sent news clippings. One from the *Chicago Daily Tribune* in 1906 shocked and saddened her. Eli Gage, aged 39, had shot himself in a third-rate hotel room in Seattle. Sophy and a woman reported to be Eli's mother had come looking for him. Martha knew Eli's mother had died when he was seven and his stepmother had died in 1901. The mother in question must have been Sophy's mother.

There was a great deal of speculation as to why the son of a wealthy and famous banker took his own life. He had been in Seattle for three weeks, staying first in the fashionable Greystone guest house. When he moved to the Tourist Hotel, he registered under a false name. Although he had been working for a plumbing supply company, he was applying for a job with the Northwestern Steamship Company at the time of his death. Four empty whisky bottles showed that he had been drinking heavily.

Where had his life gone wrong? Had his Yukon quest failed him? He was there before the stampede; saw the first gold come down the Yukon. He came home to Chicago in the fall of '97 warning of the starvation winter to come. The *Chicago Tribune* and the *Los Angeles Herald* both carried interviews with Eli urging the military to get supplies into Dawson: he even suggested a train of 50 loaded horses to bring food over the mountains. But it seems he never worked for the N.A.T.T. Company again. In the *Chicago Tribune* article, he finds it necessary to deny "malicious falsehoods" that he was "horse-whipped" by the miners in Dawson. He and Sophy got as far as Eagle in '98 but turned back. Why? When he brought that load of whisky and hardware into Dawson in August the year before and infuriated John J. Healey, who had ordered only food supplies, did he ruin his career?

Martha's thoughts went out to Eli's father and the troubles he had had. Lyman Gage lost his first wife when Eli was seven, then his daughter Fanny; then his second wife died. In 1901, when the death of President McKinley so devastated him that he was unable to eat or sleep for several days, it was Eli who came to his aid and helped him get to Buffalo to see his dying president. Now he was dealing with this tragic loss of his son.

She thought of Will, who would mourn a best friend. She thought back to the fun she and Will had at the 1893 wedding of Eli and Sophy, and the good times they had at their beautiful house in Evanston near Chicago, and the excitement in the Gage family when gold was found in the Yukon. Now it all seemed so sad and so far away.

When Christmas came in 1906, Martha invited as many "homeless" as the house could hold for Christmas dinner. On Christmas Eve, her family came home from Roman Catholic midnight mass to find their pup had pulled the tree over and torn the parcels. Friends helped them redecorate and finally left in the wee hours of morning, and by then her excited boys were awake and there was no hope of sleep. The family ate breakfast and went to the Anglican church service. Just as they had taken their pew, the fire bell rang. Government House was on fire. The Anglican church emptied, Martha's boys leading the charge to the fire.

Government House had been built only five years ago, in 1901, an ornate mansion that the papers called "the finest home structure in the Yukon." It had already been touched by tragedy when James Hamilton Ross, third Commissioner of the Yukon, was living there. Mrs. Ross was making a trip out on the S.S. *Islander* to buy furniture for Government House. She had her little daughter with her as well as her niece. The luxurious ship was filled with passengers and was heavily loaded with gold. Forty lives were lost when the ship sank near Juneau, among them Mrs. Ross and the children. It was believed that the ship struck an iceberg, which punctured it on the forward port side. Commissioner Ross was so distraught that people feared he would not survive. He left the Yukon and, while recovering outside, was elected the first Yukon member of Parliament.

As the Dawson youngsters gathered to watch the fire engine douse the flames and George huddled with other councilors discussing the loss of their grand house, Martha remember she still had a Christmas dinner to host.

The police soon discovered that the fire had been arson. It had been deliberately set by a thief to cover his tracks. Somehow the guilty party eluded police all winter and in early spring was making his escape by steamer. Martha was on that same steamer, going out to consult with her father about selling the sawmill. As they moved up the river, a passenger named Kennedy asked Martha to read his girlfriend's palm. Out of boredom, she agreed. What she saw in the lines of the girl's hand was that someone close to her would meet a violent end in three days, or months, or years.

Three days later, the steamer arrived in Whitehorse. As Kennedy got off the boat, the Mounted Police arrested him on a charge of arson. Kennedy asked for a drink of water, grabbed a pellet of poison from his coat, swallowed it and died.

There was one other incident in her life that involved palm reading. At a reception in Chicago in the fall of 1897, a palmist from India wanted to read her hands. He told her that she would leave the country within the year. She would go to a foreign land, where she would face danger, sorrow and privation. She would give birth to another child, "a girl or an unusually devoted son."[21]

Martha presents the two stories as events that happened without saying what she believed about palmistry, but after the Kennedy incident she said she never read anyone's palms again.

There was very little crime in Dawson, but one occurrence did involve Martha and Donald. On a January night, with the thermometer at 60 below, a gray fog over the town, and the street deserted, two men barged through the back door of the Dominion Saloon brandishing a Winchester rifle and a Colt six-shooter. They emptied tills and cash drawers and robbed the few patrons and the saloon girls.

The fog covered their escape, but attempting to get out of Dawson in mid-winter would probably be a death sentence. Within a few days, the police had one of the robbers, a tall man named Tommerlin. His short partner, named Brophy, was still on the loose. To get a lesser sentence, Tommerlin "ratted" on his partner. The "law of the Yukon" did not like a double-crossing partner, so there was enough sympathy for Brophy that the Mounties were not finding him.

Martha, still living at Millhouse, was finishing her breakfast dishes when the door opened and a man entered furtively. She asked him what he wanted and he answered, "Food. Only food." He said he had had nothing to eat for three days.

Donald appeared and peppered him with questions. Martha ordered her son out of the room and back to his school work, and quickly wrapped up food for the man. She gave him bread, butter, ham, tea and sugar. "I am not sure who you are, and I don't want to know. But now that you are warm and well fed, take my advice and mush on."[22]

As he thanked her and left, the look he gave her haunted her for days.

She was roused out of bed that night by a loud knock on her door. She opened it to a Mounted Police officer, who wanted her keys to search the assay office and quartz mill.

Donald, also roused out of bed, whispered, "Will they get the man?"

"What man, son?"

"Brophy, the holdup man, Mother. He stayed in our old Carmichael cabin two nights … but I won't tell."[23]

Brophy was captured at the old Stockade Roadhouse on Bonanza Creek. He was given a life sentence, while his partner was sent back to the United States with no jail sentence. Brophy never told the hiding place of his share of the loot.

There was so much flamboyance in Dawson that a quiet bank clerk whose poetry was taking the outside world by storm, could go mostly unnoticed in his home town. Dawsonites might recite his *Cremation of Sam McGee* or *The Shooting of Dan McGrew* and have a good laugh, but the drama Robert Service wrote about was all around them, everyday stuff. Some even knew that a man named Doc Sudgen actually did cremate a body in a boiler, not on Lake Laberge but on Tagish Lake in 1899.

No one thought to invite Service to the gala celebrations being planned for the Governor General in the summer of 1909. Lord and Lady Aberdeen, their daughter Sybil, her friend the Honourable Miss Middleton, and their staff arrived in the evening and were scarcely settled in Government House when His Excellency was asking for Robert Service. A message was sent to the poet's cabin, and he was

Dredges like this one tore up creeks in Yukon and Alaska to extract the gold that early miners, with primitive equipment, had missed. Photo: Gord Mallory.

invited to breakfast. Service came with autographed copies of *Songs of a Sourdough*, which he presented to the two young ladies.

After this royal recognition, Dawsonites looked at their bank clerk in a new light. About this time, Service found the courage to quit his job. He looked in his bank book and saw that he was making five times as much money in royalties as his salary at the bank. He resigned and settled into his cabin to write *The Trail of '98*, his novel of the Gold Rush.

By 1909, dredges had changed Klondike mining. A dredge dug its own pond to sit in. First the topsoil had to be blown off with high-pressure hoses. Then, after the newly exposed layer thawed, the dredge's bucket could haul up the sediment, even bite into the bedrock. Inside the dredge, coarse gravel and rocks were removed while fine sand and gold were passed through a screen and flushed through sluice boxes, where the gold was captured by riffles and coco-matting.

Joe Boyle had been quick to see that 10 to 12 men could do the work of hundreds with the aid of a mechanical monster that stood three stories high and clanged and shrieked as it bit into bedrock. For a time, Boyle was known as King of the Yukon. He would become a hero in World War I and never return to the Yukon. After a series of strokes, he would die alone in London.

While on the Yukon Council, George worked to protect the rights of the individual miner. He had been one himself and knew how hard they worked. In 1906, he helped MP Dr. Alfred Thompson draft the Yukon Placer Mining Act to protect the rights of miners. A man named Treadgold had secured a concession from Ottawa that all lapsed Yukon claims would revert to him. Miners rose up in indignation, and the government canceled the concession and sent an Ontario judge to investigate corruption in Yukon mining. George also drew up the Miners and Woodsmens' Lien Ordinances, to protect miners and loggers whose bosses often honoured other creditors first, leaving no money to pay the workers.

Later, the Guggenheims, with their Yukon Gold Company, controlled dredge mining in the Yukon. Their concessions were not all bad for independent miners. The company had to buy a man's claim outright for $1000 or pay him 8% royalty on the gold they took out. That meant he could sit in Vancouver or Los Angeles and earn money from his Yukon claim. Some miners who never struck pay dirt received big money later from royalties because the dredges could dig deeper.

Dredge mining left deep scars in the valleys as the machines dug down as much as 60 to 79 feet to extract the gold. Ugly ditches ran down the hills to bring water to the dredges. Great heaps of gravel tailings were left behind as the operation moved up the creek. Dredges changed forever the romance of the early miners taking out their gold with pick and shovel and transporting it on the backs of their mules.

As the population of Dawson began to wane, George Black found that the town was overstocked with lawyers. George decided they should spend a year in Vancouver, where he could study and take the law examinations of British Columbia as insurance against the future. In the fall of 1909, they closed their house and took the last boat out of Dawson.

1912-1916
First Lady of the Yukon

MARTHA IS SPEEDING through the Fraser River canyon on a railway track car. She and her driver left Yale in the early hours of this June morning. She is surrounded by grandeur. Mountain streams cascade down rock walls to join the whirling Fraser River. A soft breeze stirs the scent of flowers and fir trees. Silently she offers a prayer of thanks. "Oh God, how good it is to live! How wonderful are Thy creations! How small a thing am I!"[24]

She has been given a mission—to gather and mount wild flowers of the Rocky Mountains for the Canadian Pacific Railway. She is like a dog with a bone, unable to believe in her good luck.

Before she left the Yukon, Martha had competed in a flower competition. The Yukon government offered a prize of two hundred dollars for the winning exhibit of native wild flowers. Martha had been studying the flowers of Yukon and Alaska since she first set foot on the mud of Dyea. She was often invited to speak on the subject at church gatherings, at teas and sewing circles, and, to illustrate her talks, she had learned to press and mount her flowers on watercoloured backgrounds. Martha called her hobby "artistic botany" and spent many happy hours doing it.

The contest appealed to her at once, and she planned her strategy. She wanted to have as many varieties as she could find. She would mount not just the flower but the whole plant. She would make her exhibit attractive and artistic. She was determined to win.

It seemed that everyone wanted to help. Her children and their pals took to the hills. Friends appeared with beautiful or unusual blooms. Sourdoughs from the creeks knocked at her door and proffered specimens. Some of the miners had intimate knowledge of the hills and valleys they worked on, and they knew what grew where. Sometimes they had local names for the flowers, or sometimes they actually knew the Latin names.

One who knew all the flowers by their Latin names was Frank Berton. Frank had graduated from the University of New Brunswick as a civil engineer and was offered a position at Queen's University but chose the gold rush instead. Frank had arrived in Dawson one day ahead of Martha's party. He failed to strike it rich, but the Yukon captivated him and he stayed to labor in the gold fields and eventually become Dawson's mining recorder. Martha would get to know him when he married school teacher Laura Thompson. Since Frank knew the Latin names of 300 Yukon wild flowers, he and Martha could have some good discussions on the name of a moss or the classification of a fern.

Martha made a display of 464 varieties. She fashioned a harp using four-leaf clovers and making the strings of fine, strong grasses. She made a heart of pink and white immortelles (dried everlasting flowers). When she won the prize, her display went to the World's Fair in Seattle.

Now in Vancouver, Martha had occasion to meet Mrs. Hayter Reed, whose husband was general manager of Canadian Pacific Hotels.

|| OPPOSITE: *Martha on a Yukon mountain finding wild flowers. Yukon Archives 003360.*

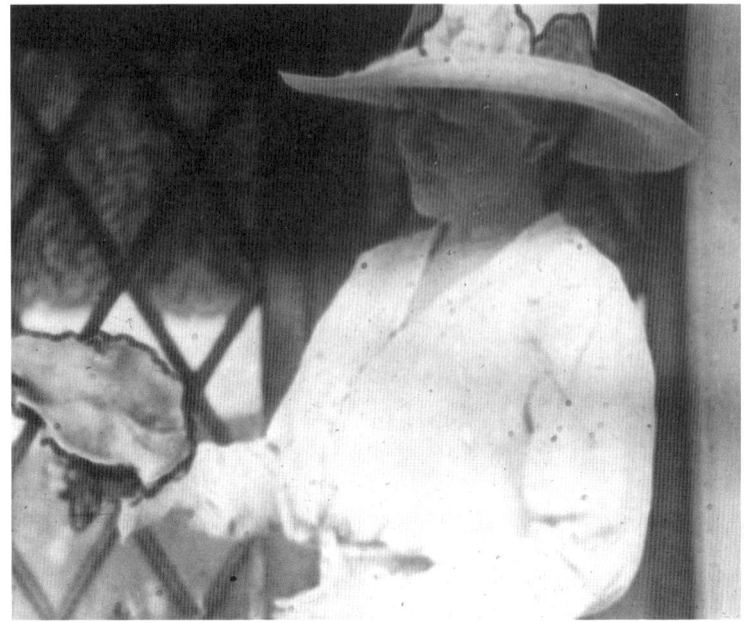

To Martha, every flower and fungus was a work of art. In the Yukon and later, in the Rocky Mountains, she collected, studied and displayed her "artistic botany." Several of her flower specimens are now in the Herbarium of Ottawa's Museum of Nature. Dawson City Museum, 1994.15.3.25.

Kate Reed was a talented decorator who travelled across Canada choosing the décor for the hotels and mountain lodges of the CPR. She had an unerring eye for luxury and a sense of Canadian history. Martha invited her to lunch and put out her place cards of Yukon pressed flowers. The two women were soon talking of art and flowers and Martha's winning exhibit of Yukon flowers. It occurred to Mrs. Reed that floral exhibits might add grace to railway hotels, and before long Martha was invited to travel through the Rockies, collecting and mounting wild flowers to be displayed in Canadian Pacific Railway stations and in their grand hotels.

She took the boys to a friend's farm at Thunder Bay, Ontario, left George studying for his law exams in Vancouver and embarked on "one of the happiest missions of my life."[25]

Her little party on the track car travelled over the Yale Creek bridge, passed through tunnels and around corners at breakneck speed with the Fraser River below them roaring through its rock walls, jumping in waves and roiling in whirlpools. Often, they were crossing water that cascaded down from the mountains to join the river.

 As they crossed and recrossed the old Caribou Road, the railroad men told tales of that other gold rush in the 1860s. Martha listened with great interest. Some of the oldest Sourdoughs in the Yukon had been there, and she had heard their stories, too. Now this old road was covered with lush mosses and several varieties of ferns.

She kept asking her driver to stop when she saw beguiling colours close to the track. Her collecting was already underway. The men were happy to stop for an hour whenever she pleased. They lifted the car off the tracks while she followed the sight or scent of a flower. Already her guides were beginning to worry they would lose her in the forest.

Her first destination would be Sicamous, on Shuswap Lake. Here she delighted in her first scarlet Indian paintbrush; in the Yukon this flower is magenta or lemon-coloured but never red. Within four miles of Sicamous, she collected two hundred specimens. A good omen for her expedition was the four-leaf clovers she found growing here in masses. Walking the tracks overlooking a marsh at Maro Lake, she spied bright yellow and she was off into the ditch and into the bog, following a heavenly scent to a bed of yellow orchids.

Her next stop was Glacier National Park. Here was a whole new cast of flowers at the foot of the glacier or on the high-altitude slopes: the dogtooth violet or "glacier lily," mountain larkspur and yellow columbine, carpets of heather. She often found herself distracted by butterflies, so she devised a way to catch them with a mixture of syrup and Scotch whisky. These butterflies would sometimes appear with the mounted flowers in the artwork she would later prepare.

All summer, Martha would ride and wander through the Rocky Mountains with the CPR at her beck and call. At the Field depot she studied the schedules of way freights so she could wander freely and signal the engineer with a white cloth in the centre of the track when she wanted to be picked up. The railway men worried about her, warning that she might meet tramps or animals such as bears, moose or elk that liked to use the tracks. Martha, having no fear of man or beast, carried on and met only friendly people, who often shared her excitement over an orchid find.

A four-day side trip to Emerald Lake began on a buckboard pulled by four horses. From there she embarked on a pack-horse trip to Summit Lake on the top of Burgess Pass. Her guide gave her Boy, a horse he called the best of the bunch, but to Martha's eyes, they were all sorry-looking beasts. He warned her to hang on to the pommel at a windfall or a stream. She soon discovered Boy loved to jump over any and every obstacle.

Their party climbed for six hours to Lookout Point, then descended to a camp in Yoho Valley. She was so stiff from the ride that she needed help to get off her horse, but once on solid earth she was soon hiking to Takakaw Falls and collecting flowers. After a good dinner and stories around a campfire, the whole party slept soundly in the mountain air.

Next day, they reached Wapti Glacier by noon. From there the trail got really bad, muddy with windfalls and streams, which Boy insisted on jumping. After Twin Falls, they climbed to 8500 feet and their second camp.

Martha wandered across a glacial valley to climb a slope covered with pink moss campion, yellow anemones, spring beauties, Indian paintbrush and yellow arnica. When she finally looked up from the spectacle of flowers, the sky was turning dark. Suddenly she was enveloped in a snowstorm. To get back, she could only follow the tinkle of bells on the horses and then the excited calling of her guide searching for her. Cold and soaked through, she staggered into camp, borrowed dry clothes and was revived by a hot drink and a good dinner.

Next day, the trail became really bad, narrow, rocky and slippery from rain and snow, winding along the edge of sheer cliffs. The guide had warned them to give their ponies their heads, but she worried that Boy might jump them to their deaths below.

When the field excursion was over, Martha travelled to Lake Louise, with its Arctic poppies dancing beside the turquoise lake, a jewel set in a ring of mountains. From there, she went to Banff, where she would spend three weeks. Her father joined her in Banff, and they had wonderful times hiking and exploring together until the summer ended. George Munger was retired now and living in California, but he still liked to talk about Catalpa Knob and the trees and shrubs and flowers he grew there and compare them with what he and Martha were finding here in Alberta.

Banff was interesting not only for the flowers but for the people Martha was meeting, especially two women, Mary T. Shaffer and Julia Henshaw. Mary Shaffer, from Pennsylvania, was an explorer, mountaineer, naturalist, and photographer. She had been working with her husband, Charles, on a book of mountain plants when Charles died in 1903. She decided she would have to go on alone and set out with a friend named Mollie Adams and a trusted guide, to photograph and collect plants to illustrate the botanical guide she and her husband had planned. Their book, *Alpine Flowers of the Canadian Rockies*, was published in 1907. Mary found she could not stop exploring and became a famed intrepid mountaineer. Shortly after Martha met her, she built a home in Banff and in 1915 married her trusted guide, Billy Warren.

Julia Henshaw had a great deal in common with Mary Shaffer. The two women were sometimes friends, sometimes competitors. Julia published *Mountain Wildflowers of Canada* in 1906, a year ahead of Mary's, making it the first North American guide to alpine plants. Martha found Julia's book with its colour-coded arrangement of flowers often very helpful in her own explorations.

During the rainy Vancouver winter, Martha would study her specimens and then mount them in artistic arrangements to grace the lobbies and chambers of hotels across Canada. In researching and describing the plant life she found, she never considered herself a scientific botanist, but her knowledge was extensive. Later on, her work would be displayed in the MacBride Museum in Whitehorse, in the National Herbarium of Canada and in the Parliament Buildings in Victoria.

Her work for the CPR resulted in a similar offer from the government of Belgium. This would require three years away from home. Reluctantly, she turned it down. This would be the first time she turned her back on adventure in favour of family. Donald and Lyman were 18 and 12, and they needed her attention. Warren had grown up in the care of Purdy and Munger grandparents, and although he was well looked after and well educated, she regretted the separation.

She also wanted to support George, who had thrown himself into the 1911 campaign for the federal Conservatives against the Laurier government's proposed reciprocity with the United States. The Conservatives defeated Laurier, and a year later George Black was named the seventh Commissioner of the Yukon.

Joyfully, the Black family headed north in March. While Martha had been in and out of the Yukon several times, she had not made the

Road houses like this one at Minto were situated every 15 mi (24 km) along the Overland Trail to welcome cold and hungry passengers from stagecoach or winter sleigh. Photo: Gord Mallory.

trip in winter before. From Skagway, the White Pass and Yukon Railway took them to Whitehorse; then it would be 360 miles (580 km) to Dawson by stage—a large White Pass sleigh—which she and her family shared with nine or ten other travellers.

When the White Pass and Yukon Railroad from Skagway had reached Whitehorse in 1900, steamers multiplied on the river. Newspapers now arrived in Dawson from Seattle and San Francisco. Bert Parker, who had arrived in 1898 at 18 years old and then spent seven months in Father Judge's hospital recovering from typhoid fever, made his fortune selling the *San Francisco Chronicle* in the summer of '99.

When the papers landed on the Dawson dock, he found he could sell "anywhere from five hundred to a thousand papers within an hour."[26] One gold-rich miner paid him $65 for a 25-cent paper. But when the last boat headed up the Yukon River in October, Dawson was tucked

Road signs on the Klondike Highway tell the story of the trail and the winter sleighs that travelled its 332 miles (435 km) of snow and ice. Photo: Gord Mallory.

in until spring. Mail and newspapers from the outside world would arrive only spasmodically, by dog team.

In 1902 the White Pass and Yukon Route built a 330-mile (531 km) overland trail as a mail and freight transportation route along the shore of the Yukon River. Now travelers could use its 12-foot (4 m) roughly graded surface by summer stage as an alternative to steamers. In winter, the only alternative to staying home was to wrap oneself in furs and travel by winter stage, which was a large sleigh pulled by four or six strong horses. Coonskin coats were the necessary wear; even in March, Yukon temperatures could dip to 40 below. People who went out in winter could leave their coats tagged and hung in the stage office at Whitehorse to be picked up on the way back. There were hot bricks for your feet. If the mercury showed 40 below, the stage did not run. Laura Berton said that if a thermometer was not available at a roadhouse they used Perry Davis Painkiller; if it turned to slush, the temperature was too low for travel. At road houses spaced 15 to 22 miles apart, a new team of horses would replace the spent horses and passengers would visit the outhouse, eat a big meal, thaw out and be ready to ride again.

Martha said their trip in 1912 took 10 days. "We jolted, slipped, and slid up and down steep and icy hillsides, over frozen rivers and lakes, stopping every fifteen or twenty miles at road-houses."[27] Eight miles from Dawson, a sleigh appeared with a load of friends come to welcome the Blacks back from Vancouver. Their official welcome a few days later in the A.B. Hall was a grand affair, with almost a thousand people attending. It was obvious that Dawson was bringing home their favourite family.

After the fire in 1906, Government House had been rebuilt in a less ornate but classic colonial style. It had three stories, with a large wrap-around veranda and a balcony above. White pillars graced the entrance. Inside the paneling was of British Columbia fir, the wallpaper golden, the drawing room large and elegant.

Martha immediately liked the well-planned layout of Government House, which included drawing, reception, living and dining rooms, plus a kitchen and pantry, all on the main floor. Above that were the bedrooms and writing rooms; above these, a floor for servants and a billiard room. But the house was in bad repair. She stared at cracks in the kitchen where she could see the outdoors. She set about repairing, restoring and enhancing the beauty of Government House.

She had plans for this "house of the people." She had often walked by, admiring the house and feeling sad that the common citizen, who with pick-ax and strong back had mined the gold that built it, had little access to the building. As soon as she had the house in order and had

Government House restored to the style and beauty of its early years. Here Martha reigned as chatelaine from the spring of 1912 to the fall of 1916. Photo: Enid Mallory.

hired a cook, butler, housemaid, gardener and assistant, she invited Dawson to an open house—"all who wished to come."

Her cook and butler shook their heads in disbelief as she asked them to make 1000 sandwiches, along with 20 gallons each of salads and sherbet and 40 cakes, plus gallons of punch. Friends made 20 pounds of candy and helped decorate the house. Furniture was moved, flags put up, tables laid with white cloths, which Martha adorned with red poppies and maidenhair ferns and sweet peas.

The first guest arrived before 8 p.m. At midnight, they took up the rugs and danced. The last guest left at 5 a.m. There were 600 visitors. She had set the tone for her days as chatelaine of Government House. What pleased her most was someone's remark, "The Blacks didn't have to go to Government House to learn how to entertain; they always did keep open house."[28]

First Lady of the Yukon

Martha reigned at Government House. Sometimes she was called Queen of the Yukon. American friends called her the First Lady. Robert Service, in a letter to a Clemmie Burns, described her as a Marquise. She called herself the *chatelaine*, a name meaning mistress of a chateau or sometimes used to mean ornament. She saw herself as hostess, entertainer, and perhaps, when wearing her favourite gown, an ornament.

Eudora Ferry, married to a Yukon Gold Company engineer, described Martha as a "dynamic personality" who made Dawson society "anything but provincial." She said Martha had changed Government House from a tired, run-down building to "a spacious, charming mansion, filled with handsome furniture, luxurious carpets and satisfying colour." She said Dawson could be proud it had "one of the most gifted and charming women in the country to act as chatelaine."[29]

As spring came, Martha turned her attention to the gardens. She wanted to grow food, and she wanted beauty. With her two gardeners, she transplanted raspberries, gooseberries, cranberries, currants. They enlarged the greenhouse and made a root house. In the long days of Arctic sunshine, they watched the vegetables grow incredibly fast. She admitted that the garden might not pay for itself, but the eating was really good.

Meanwhile, the flower garden became a real show-stopper. Daffodils, tulips, irises and jonquils started the show, to be followed by every flower that could grow so far north—nasturtiums, delphiniums, snapdragons and 12-foot-high sweet peas. The path behind the house was lined with poppies—California, Shirley and Oriental.

Martha even decided they should have chickens. When they stopped laying in winter, she read that a mixture of chopped meat and red pepper would make them lay again. When her cook told her that the 30 hens had laid 32 eggs in one day, she investigated. She found that

Martha delivering flowers. She made the grounds of Government House a showplace of botanical beauty and shared the bounty with Dawson citizens. Yukon Archives, Martha Louise Black fonds, 82 294 3254.

George had been buying the eggs and planting them in the nests as a joke. Her precious hens would wait until spring to lay.

There were other pranks usually involving her boys. Donald was now studying engineering at Leland Stanford University in California, under the watchful eye of Father Munger, but he came to Dawson in summer to work for the Yukon Gold Company. Financed by the New York Guggenheims, the company acquired most of the claims on Bonanza and Eldorado creeks and, like Boyle, brought in dredges and hydraulic monitors. During a party at the house for Lyman's friends, the bell of the Anglican church next door began to ring. This had happened more than once before. At least this time her boys were right here, and not the culprits. She was boasting of their innocence next day when she saw Lyman struggling not to laugh, and then he confessed,

"We tied a rope from our upstairs window to the bell and took turns ringing it."[30] When the adults had begun investigating, one of the boys had cut the rope while another hauled it off the lawn.

Martha herself got in trouble during the combined Dominion Day and Fourth of July celebration. Government House was decorated with the flags of several countries, and there was a plan to take photos at midnight and send them outside to Canadian newspapers. The revelers heard a steamer come in, and someone reported that the Seattle Chamber of Commerce was aboard and its members were coming to join the Government House gathering. When she heard this, Martha disappeared upstairs. Only a few people saw her hanging up an enormous American flag.

When the photographer developed his pictures next day to accompany the news item, "Dawson IODE Celebrated Dominion Day," there was the blatant Stars and Stripes demanding full attention. Staunch Canadians called the flag incident a brazen affront and the pictures had to have three inches cut off the top before they were sent outside.

Martha saw no problem with being an American as well as a Canadian, just as she saw no problem being a big-C Conservative and a small-l liberal. When a lawyer who was a friend of George married the dance-hall girl known as Diamond Tooth Gertie, Martha invited them to a party at Government House. She was breaking an unspoken rule in Dawson that dance-hall girls were not invited to social occasions. That Gertie Lovejoy was entertained at Government House caused shock waves among her IODE friends.

Martha had established Dawson's first chapter of the IODE in 1913. The Imperial Order Daughters of the Empire was founded in 1900 as a patriotic organization to support Canadians fighting for the Empire in South Africa. Martha may have been influenced by her

Rocky Mountain flowers friend, Julia Henshaw, who was active in the organization. The new Dr. George M. Dawson chapter was named after the pioneer geologist who explored the Yukon area. It would become an important structure in the social life of Dawson and would play a major role in the difficult times ahead.

Meanwhile, George was working to improve life for Yukoners. One of his first concerns was the Overland Trail, always in need of money for its upkeep. Ruts and gopher holes had to be filled. Sections had to be rerouted around mud slides or fallen boulders or places where permafrost melted and turned the roadbed to soup.

As automobiles began to appear in the Yukon, road condition took on new importance. The Yukon Council was asking Ottawa for $50,000. In Ottawa, MPs argued that the Yukon's winter temperature was too low for automobiles, and in summer the terrain was too muddy or too rough. A recent attempt by Joe Boyle to travel from Dawson to Whitehorse in a Flanders car had failed.

George talked the Yukon Gold Company's manager, C.A. Thomas, into trying it in his 40-horsepower auto between Christmas and New Years of 1912. Martha and the boys waved them off, the two men and their chauffeur bundled in coonskin coats, the thermometer dropping lower each day and daylight limited to a few hours at noon. The car had one headlight.

Snow would smooth the worst rough places, but it was a risky 350 miles (563 km) ahead. Even today, the North Klondike Highway in winter is dangerous. If your car quits or you run out of gas, you can freeze to death. In 1912, their open vehicle would have been much like the winter stage, except that horses don't break down or get flat tires.

When travel writer Frank G. Carpenter arrived in Dawson in 1916, he interviewed George and they talked about that trip. Carpenter reported that their average speed was 20 miles (32 km) per hour. At one roadhouse, they learned that the thermometer had dropped to 56 below, but their furs had kept them warm. Keeping the engine warm was another matter; if they stopped, it would freeze and the oil would congeal.

They were 20 miles (32 km) from a roadhouse when they ran out of gas. "A dog team was found and sent on to the road house, but while they waited, the engine froze and the oil became stiff. They had to build a fire under the car with wood from the forest before they could start off again. When they had completed the journey and returned to Dawson, the bill for the road appropriation was just coming up for action. The news of their trip was telegraphed to Ottawa and the bill was passed."[31]

The Blacks had two idyllic years at Government House before their world changed. On August 4, 1914, they were enjoying an evening at the Auditorium Theatre when a telegram arrived for George. He went to the stage and told Dawson that Great Britain was now at war with Germany. There was a sudden silence as a shock wave went through the hall, then the 20 members of the Mounted Police who were present rose to their feet to sing "God Save the King," and the whole room belted out the anthem.

Life in Dawson changed. Men who had left everything to get to the Klondike now left whatever they had here to get to the war. Some left on steamer or stage; some walked. "With packs on their backs they mushed from two to four hundred miles."[32]

Joe Boyle, the man who brought mechanical mining into Dawson, whose giant dredges had upturned seven miles of the Klondike River and made millions for himself, lost no time in organizing and financing a machine gun battery of 50 men who would be part of the Canadian Expeditionary Force.

The women of Dawson girded themselves for war work. Julia Henshaw, now national president of the IODE, contacted the Dawson chapter for help in raising funds to equip a hospital ship. Yukon women sprang into action. In four days, they collected more than $6,000.

Martha threw her house open for friends to sew and knit for the war. Her spacious rooms were made available for bake sales, entertainment and dances to raise money. Meanwhile, Martha was taking St. John's Ambulance courses in first aid.

From his post at Government House, George Black watched the Yukon men march off to war. Finally, at the end of 1915, he could stand it no longer. He told Martha he had to enlist, and she did not try to stop him. From the time they married, she and George seemed to be on the same page.

George resigned as Commissioner and set about to organize a Yukon Infantry Company. First in line to join George's company was Lyman, just turning 17. Like so many other boys, he would lie about his age in order to enlist.

Martha's oldest son, Warren, was a graduate of Annapolis Naval Academy and was to command a troop ship in the Pacific. Donald, finishing his course at Stanford University, would be granted his degree early so he could enlist if the United States entered the war.

All her men were going to war. What was Martha to do?

"Follow them!"[33]

OPPOSITE: *Seventeen-year-old Lyman poses with his mother on steps of school before going off to war. Yukon Archives 78 112 1.*

FOLLOWING PAGES: *Martha and George in conversation at home in Government House. Dawson City Museum, 2001.23.02.*

1916-1919
Mother to Yukon Soldiers

IN OCTOBER 1915, George and Martha made a trip "outside" to see loved ones before committing themselves to war. They went first to Ottawa, so George could talk about resigning as Commissioner to raise another Yukon company and obtaining his commission as captain to lead them. They visited George's relatives and spent some time in Toronto, where Martha met with Mrs. E. Johnson, national president of the IODE. Martha then spent the winter with her family in California while George trained in Victoria to qualify as captain of the Yukon company to be known as the 104th Regiment. Back in Dawson, volunteers, including Lyman and several of his school friends, were training in the Arctic Brotherhood Hall. Of the 255 volunteers, 17 were American-born.

Meanwhile, George had been stricken with appendicitis. He had surgery at the Royal Jubilee Hospital in Victoria and developed serious complications. He was finally recovering by the end of May and headed north, still very frail. He and Martha returned to Dawson on the *Casa* on June 8.

On June 9, the *Casa* left Dawson carrying the first 120 men of the Yukon Infantry Company. One of them was Lyman. As Martha watched the little steamer with its red paddlewheel and yellow smokestack disappear around the bend, she wondered what was in store for all of them.

George suffered a relapse and was not well enough to speak at Dawson's July 1st celebration, so Martha took his place. She told her audience:

"The Great War is a woman's war as well as a man's war. When peace comes, the articles of peace will affect the women quite as vitally as they will affect the men, so that while we, because of our very sex, are not called upon to bear arms in a physical sense, yet we are daily called upon to bear the brunt of many a battle."[34]

When Martha announced her intention to go, her IODE friends formed a Martha Munger Black Chapter and established the Yukon Comfort Fund (Martha's idea), the money collected to be used specifically for Yukon boys overseas.

Martha had moved house many times by 1916, but leaving her beautiful Government House was the saddest departure. She had been so happy here. She had been Dawson's leading lady, and she was giving up her stage.

On October 9, 275 men and boys under Captain George Black embarked on the *Casa*, with Martha the only woman aboard. All of Dawson was out to cheer them on. As the *Casa* prepared to leave, a brass band on shore played "When the Ice Worms Nest Again." The Yukon version ended:

> There's a land of midnight sun,
> Where Boyle's dredges groan and hum,
> And the ptarmigan are warbling in the trees.
> And the whisky that they sell

Mother to Yukon Soldiers

Make you wish you were in—well,
Our thoughts will float to you on every breeze."[35]

Martha was also being sent off like a heroine. She was presented with a poke of gold nuggets, one from each member of the IODE chapter. Martha would keep these all her life in case she ever fell upon hard times. The boys had been given sewing kits and socks and large supplies of tobacco and candy. They thanked Dawson with a poem that ended,

We have stolen Mrs. Black,
and we will not bring her back
Till the Germans quit, and when the Allies win,
Till we nail the Union Jack on the Kaiser's chimney stack,
And we toast the Yukon daughters in Berlin.[36]

On their voyage to Victoria, Martha had the men busy tearing white linette into five-inch squares for a quilt. Each man would autograph a square to be sent back to Dawson and put together in a quilt to be raffled off. A thousand tickets were sold to raise money for the war. In March 1917, a little three-year-old girl drew the winning ticket—and Martha Black was the winner.

The Yukon Infantry Company trained at Willows Camp in Victoria. Before Lyman was sworn in, he and George officially changed his name to Lyman Black, the name he had called himself for years. While the men were training, Martha enrolled in first-aid courses. Martha dipped into the Yukon Comfort Fund to provide a sumptuous Christmas dinner for the Yukon boys.

A man could march off to war with cheers and blessings, but Martha discovered a woman had to fight her way there. Sitting in Victoria

On board the S.S. Canada, Martha and George with the ship's captain, on their way to war. Dawson City Museum, 1994.15.2.26.

trying to deal with authorities in Ottawa was getting her nowhere. George's company had orders to "stand by" and would be heading to Halifax. With time running out, Martha boarded a train to Ottawa. She went first to Sir Douglas Hazen, Minister of Marine, who had been her guest at Government House in Dawson. She even scored an interview with Prime Minister Sir Robert Borden. They told her she could go only if General Bigger agreed. Bigger was Officer Commanding Transportation at Halifax.

Off Martha went to Halifax. Bigger suggested she would not want to be the only woman aboard a ship with 2000 men. Martha replied that she had walked over the Chilkoot Pass with thousands of men who did her no harm.

"We'll see!" was the best she got.

The Yukon men arrived. She watched Lyman board the S.S. *Canada* while George went to General Bigger for orders. Martha waited hours in suspense for George's return. He greeted her with a smile. "Well, you can go."

George told her the rest of the story. Bigger had waited to talk to George. "I have held back permission until I found out from you personally if you really want her. Some husbands prefer their wives to stay at home."[37]

If Martha had not been so happy just then, she would have been furious at the man.

They had a rough crossing. One of the lads was seriously ill, and George had him moved to a cabin next to theirs so Martha could help nurse him. Seasick herself, she managed to sew two pneumonia jackets to help him. There were no antibiotics in World War I. The only treatment for pneumonia was fluids and rest and these jackets to warm the chest. They were made of oiled silk or muslin or sometimes of rubber tubing, which contained hot water like a hot-water bottle. Already Martha was glad of the first-aid courses she had taken in Dawson and Victoria.

Their voyage was so stormy that they were unable to keep the other troopships and the convoy destroyer in sight. Crossing the Atlantic in January 1917 was a dangerous undertaking. In the distance they saw a blazing ship and learned that the *Floridian* had been torpedoed. The S.S. *Canada's* luck held, and they reached Liverpool in eight days. Martha watched her men go off to an "unknown training camp." Then she took a train to London and the Savoy Hotel, where George and Lyman would find her when they had landing leave.

Next day, she went to the office of the Red Cross to volunteer. She was assigned to the Prisoners-of-War Department, where she typed letters all day. She had her reunion with George and Lyman. Both were being transferred to a machine gun unit. George had chosen to revert to Lieutenant in order to see action sooner.

Yukoners were made welcome in London. Joe Boyle's machine gun battery had preceded them and distinguished themselves in battle. Newspapers were telling how 10 percent of the Yukon population had come 8000 miles to fight for "King and Country." George was welcomed as Commissioner of the Yukon, Martha as First Lady. They were given cards of admission to the Distinguished Visitor's Gallery, Martha to a top-storey Ladies Gallery behind an iron grille. She remarked to members later that men here were so frightened of women that they kept them behind bars.

Wherever Martha went, she found friends, new and old. The Duke and Duchess of Connaught invited the Blacks to dinner. From 1911 to 1916, they had lived in Rideau Hall in Ottawa, the Duke being the first member of the royal family to be Governor General of Canada. While in Canada they had planned a visit to Dawson, which had to be canceled when war broke out. As early as 1914 the Duchess was raising money to establish military hospitals in Europe for wounded men of the Canadian Expeditionary Force. While the Yukon women were busy collecting $6000 for a hospital ship, the Duchess donated $1000 to the IODE campaign.

The incoming mayor of London, Sir Charles Hanson, had been a Canadian businessman. He invited the Blacks to see the Lord Mayor's procession from the balcony of Mansion House. In April, when the United States entered the war, they were invited to the service of commemoration in St. Paul's Cathedral. They sat near the royal party, and Martha recorded what Queen Mary wore—a grey tailored suit and a black satin sailor hat with an upturned brim and a high osprey feather.

Such happy occasions were outweighed by weeks and months of gloom and anxiety and long hours of hard work. She had moved now to a small, dismal flat. Often, she wasn't well. She endured two bouts of appendicitis and for two weeks was laid low with rheumatic fever. While everyone asked her about the Yukon cold, Martha said she was colder here than she had ever been at home. How she longed for a Klondike stove. You could not get warm at a tiny grate containing a handful of coal.

The other question asked was where in the world was the Yukon. Martha heard that a nurse preparing a comatose patient for surgery answered, "Probably somewhere in China." The patient, who was a Sourdough, sprang up in bed and yelled, "Hell! Yukon is in Canada … near the North Pole!"[38]

Martha's most important role in London was being Mother Yukon. Early on, some of the soldiers of the Yukon Company were delegated to ask if they could call her "Mother." Many of them were really still boys and often in need of mother love, sympathy and advice. Martha dispensed it all while holding "open house" in the small flat she rented.

One man wanted to know what to do because he had married an English girl and had a child but he also had a wife and two more children back in Canada. Martha advised him to volunteer for the front line and die for his country.

Letters came to her from the trenches. "I'm in a semi-dugout, like a camp of the most careless and shiftless prospector who ever went North."[39] The letters asked for chewing tobacco and socks for feet that were always wet and cold. In the spring, soldiers pressed daffodils and violets inside their letters to her. When on leave, they visited her in her flat and she fed them home-cooked meals. Their chatter helped to cheer her when she did not know where her own boys were. She had heard that Warren had been ordered to Bangkok, Siam, to escort a captured German ship to San Francisco. She did not know whether Donald was overseas or not.

When new regulations made the POW work more difficult and sporadic, Martha kept busy doing canteen work for the YMCA, sewing for the Red Cross, acting as a correspondent for the *Dawson News* and the *Whitehorse Star*, shopping for the Yukon Comfort Fund, and distributing care parcels sent from Dawson. Led by the IODE, Dawson women were indefatigable throughout the war. At social get-togethers, athletic events, political rallies and theatricals, they raised money for the war.

Martha was also spending one day a week at Battersea social housing with wives and mothers of disabled soldiers, helping them write applications for pensions, then writing reports and recommendations to the government. She became very close to some of these women, concerned that their children had adequate food and clothing, and hiring one of the mothers as her char-lady.

There were dark, rainy days when her spirits were very low. She had never worked harder in her life, but was she making any difference to the men in the thick of it? One day, she lashed out at a woman in a "beautiful satin dress trimmed with real fur." The woman was complaining about poor food and difficult servants. Martha was dressed in old clothes and "'ugly English boots," and was never at her best when not nicely dressed.

Her happy days were when George or Lyman had leave. She and George visited the sights of London together. There were two wonderful weeks when Lyman had his first leave from the front. "He's grown like a weed, loves his work, and never forgets he is a soldier." She saw that war had changed the boy who left the Yukon at 17. "He looks twenty-nine instead of nineteen."[40]

Each time she shared those good days with George or Lyman, she had to let them go, turn back to her dreary flat and wonder if she would see them again.

Mother to Yukon Soldiers

Hospital visits were always difficult. Seeing Yukon men and boys disfigured or lacking limbs brought her up against the horrid reality of war. She received a message that a Yukon soldier in hospital at Willesden wanted to see her. Her guide book told her to take Bus 8. Bus 8 was full, and she stood holding a heavy burning bush she had bought for him. When she finally got a seat, two nurses ahead of her were talking about hospital visitors who were stupid enough to bring flowers instead of fruit or cigarettes.

Hours later, at Willesden, she was directed to walk right one block, then left three or four to a field. She reached the field in a downpour and plodded across, fearful that there might be a bull among the cows. Four hours after leaving home, she arrived at the hospital. The patient was overjoyed to see her and admired his plant. But before she left, he said, "Mother, would you mind very much if I gave this plant to one of the sisters? It's her birthday, and every other fellow in the ward has given her a present, but nothing as swell as this. And she just loves flowers." Then he exclaimed, "Here she is now."[41]

Martha turned around to find herself staring at one of the nurses who had sat ahead of her on the bus. All she could do was wish her "Happy birthday" and try not to laugh as the sister walked away with the heavy burning bush.

Another role Martha played in London was ambassador and travel agent. She had carted boxes of glass slides across the Atlantic and was soon giving talks on her beloved Yukon to raise money for war efforts. For months she gave lectures almost daily: *The Romance of the Yukon Gold Fields* or *A Trip to Klondyke* or *Canada* or *A Talk on the States*. Her slides showed them the Yukon; her stories took them over the Chilkoot or White Pass, down the Yukon River and up the creeks where men moiled for gold. She took them on eight-day trips on the

Overland Stage at 30 below. She told them about Yukon wildlife, birds and flowers.

Her longest and most exhausting lecture tour was a three-week journey to Wales. Its beauty sometimes reminded her of Yukon terrain. She was billeted at all sorts of houses and had to catch trains while carrying heavy slides and equipment as well as her suitcase of clothing.

One time, at Church House in London, she spoke on Missionaries of the Yukon. She was pinch-hitting for Bishop Stringer of the Yukon, who could not be there. She was introduced as an afterthought and called a Sourdough.

She rose to speak and said, "My Lord Chairman, my lords, ladies, and gentlemen, if this be the way you usually treat women who are invited to address you, I do not wonder suffragettes go around with axes over here." (She was referring to suffragette Mary Leigh, who actually threw a hatchet at Prime Minster Henry Asquith.)

The bishop rose to speak, but Martha stopped him. "My Lord, several times in London I have had to listen to you without interrupting when I should have very much liked to do so. Now please listen to me without interruption." The audience applauded.

In her speech, she spoke of married life and her belief in harmony in religion, politics and country. "And so, because I married an Anglican, I am one. But had I married a Fiji Islander, I would probably be eating missionary now instead of talking missionary."

Afterward, as a group of them stood talking with the bishop, a woman who had been shocked at her speech said that surely she would not eat missionaries. Martha said, "Well—I did feel like taking a bite out of his lordship."[42] The bishop had a good sense of humour and laughed heartily at this.

In June 1917, Martha became a fellow of the Royal Geographical Society, recognized for her collection of Yukon flora displayed at the

Seattle Exposition, and for her work with the CPR collecting mountain flora in British Columbia.

One day, Joe Boyle appeared in Martha's kitchen as she was making dinner for some Yukon boys on leave. He told her such amazing stories that she "nearly sugared the gravy."

Joe Boyle was a larger-than-life Yukon character. He had arrived in Skagway with Frank Slavin of boxing fame in 1897, already out of money. They became a vaudeville team; Frank could box and Joe could sing and play the banjo. When they reached Dawson, they started a steam laundry. For a time, Martha's brother George managed Joe's laundry business.

Joe saw the possibilities for hydraulicking and dredging replacing the toil of placer mining. He managed to talk the Canadian government into a concession of 40 square miles of mining land, and he talked investors into cold cash for the equipment. When he left all this behind to join the war, he was sent to Russia. After the revolution there, he was given the task of retrieving Romania's treasures, which had been deposited with the Kremlin for safekeeping. By now, Romania was beset on all sides by enemies, its citizens facing starvation. Joe managed to get food supplies through and later to arrange a $25 million credit from Canada, through which he distributed food to feed Romanians after the war. King Ferdinand and Queen Marie proclaimed him the "Saviour of Romania." He was also a great favourite at Buckingham Palace. Queen Marie was a cousin of George V and British royals were grateful for his protection of her and her people.

Sometime after Joe's visit, Queen Marie herself arrived in London. She was always a welcome guest at Buckingham Palace. Because she wanted to thank Canadians for Joe Boyle's help, one hundred Canadians, George and Martha included, were invited by Sir George and Lady Perley, High Commissioner for Canada, to be presented to Queen

Martha, in her hat and her "ugly English boots", sits down, aims and shoots. Yukon Archives, George Black fonds, 81_107_53.

Marie. Martha knew Joe Boyle as a Yukon friend, but in conversation with Queen Marie on that occasion and others, Martha understood that she loved and worshiped Joe Boyle.

Martha, who described Marie as a poised, regal queen with golden brown hair and blue-black eyes, never failed to note what royalty wore. Queen Marie had a sable cape lined with ermine and a sable muff edged in ermine. Her gown was panne velvet, the skirt *en traine*, and its side panels had sable borders. She wore a silver turban with gold and bronze flowers.

Sometimes Martha was able to travel to Witley Camp in Sussex, where George was still waiting with his men to be sent into action. She was there on July 10, 1917, and was photographed in position to shoot a gun. The picture appeared in the *Dawson Daily News* in June 1919. At least two Dawson soldiers remembered her visit. Harold Butler recorded the event in a letter home:

Last week we marched to Aldershot, to the ranges where all the big machine targets are. We enjoyed a pleasant surprise when Mrs. Black arrived on the ranges, and, when through shooting, Mrs. Black, like a real machine gun No. 1, sat herself down behind the gun and let go, and made a very high score.[43]

John Chambers also wrote home:

Well, she sat down to the gun, laid it on the target, tapped it into correct position, and first burst, down goes all the ranging plates; second, taps the gun onto the target and blazes away 75 times and puts 64 on the bull. I never saw anything like it for a beginner. She seemed to be right at home.[44]

Perhaps Martha was not altogether a beginner. She had been on many a hunting foray with George.

In London, air raids punctuated her days; altogether, she endured 12 of them. "Fire engines are tearing up and down. Sirens are screaming. The London searchlights, huge phantom fingers, not unlike northern lights without colour, are sweeping the sky, making it as light as day."[45]

Her spirits hit rock bottom when Lyman was reported missing in March 1918. A letter from George said he was unable to get news of him. He knew his unit was away to the south, and the news from there was not good. He told Martha he was fearfully worried about their son. After a week of despair, she had news that he had been found and was being hailed a hero. How she longed to be back home with George, with Donald and Lyman playing teenage pranks, and her Yukon friends around her. But here she was, and the war dragged on.

Later a friend wrote to Martha, telling her some of Lyman's story during the time George reported him missing. He was with Joe Boyle's

In March of 1918, Yukon troops moved to the Western Front, where they were part of a major offensive against the German line. Yukon Archives, George Black fonds, 81_107_163.

Yukon Motor Machine Gun Battery on March 21, 1918, when the Germans launched an offensive at Amiens. Two days later, as they moved their guns from Vimy south to Amiens, the Battery suffered terrible casualties.

> During the night the infantry fell back without telling the machine gunners. … We retreated a quarter of a mile to a better position.
> While retreating Sergeant Blaikie and Private Fisher fell, Lyman stopped to see if he could help them, but Blaikie was dead and Fisher, who was dying, urged him to save himself. As the Huns were right on our heels he had to run for it. He then remounted the one remaining gun and opened up on them. For twelve days he was in fighting like this, and how he ever came through without a scratch is a marvel. Much of the time he was

cut off from his O.C. [officer in charge] and was entirely on his own.[46]

British and Australian machine gunners replaced Lyman's men on April 3. But on April 4, they were ordered back into action as the Germans attacked the village of Villers-Bretonneux. There Lyman saw a German shell hit soldiers who were unloading ammunition from a truck. The explosion killed 30 of his comrades, leaving him without a machine gun crew. Lyman later described that battle to George, and George passed on his story in a letter to Martha:

> *There was a perfectly good armoured car standing there fully equipped, guns, ammunition and crew, so I hopped on to it and out the road we went between the lines on a good road in 'no man's land' that the enemy was advancing at right angles to in bunches. Before they realized what was coming we were onto them pouring in burst after burst of machine gun fire annihilating a group here and a group there and back to our lines without a man getting hit. The other cars were then put at the same work and did mighty well. This was the first time a Canadian armoured machine gun car was taken into the scrapping and made to do the work for which it was designed. It was swell fun, the best I ever had in my life.*

George Black must have shuddered at the reckless audacity of youth as he heard his son describe the fighting as *fun*. But he finished his letter with a profession of pride in his son: "He is some great kid and certainly ought to get a decoration, his stories read like a Henty book, after they have been picked out of him word by word."[47]

Another friend wrote to Martha of the event:

> *The O.C. says that boy of yours is a perfect wizard with motor lorries and cycles—a born organizer, as brave as a lion, and sometimes 'a damned little fool for running into danger.' But he and his battery have made the Yukon name immortal, for I hear it was the machine guns that saved the day.*[48]

George's 17th Machine Gun Company had been sent to Europe in March 1918. In August, the telegram she had dreaded every day of her time in London arrived. George was wounded at the Battle of Amiens.

> *Sincerely regret to inform you Captain George Black, Infantry, officially reported admitted to Stationary Hospital, Abbeville, 11th August—gunshot wound—thigh.*[49]

Then came a letter from George. "I am lucky," he wrote. He had a chuck of shrapnel in his left leg, and a machine-gun bullet had punctured his right leg. He felt lucky to be alive. He had seen his comrades fall and die with no luck at all.

His unit had been ordered "to be a link between the most advanced Canadian cavalry and the leading French infantry." In the dark, with two motor machine-gun brigades, they proceeded down the Amiens-Roye road. At first, they surprised the Germans and smashed their defence. "We passed them back in droves. They seemed very willing to be taken, to let us have all their equipment, and helped us carry our dead and wounded from the field."

As they moved on, fighting was everywhere around them, in fields and valleys, along the road, in the villages they passed. On the second day they ran into heavy fire from concealed field-and-machine-gun nests and saw their own men "fall thick and fast." They came upon a road-block of trees felled by the Germans. In spite of heavy fire, their soldiers grabbed axes and cleared it, but it was here that a sniper bullet found George's leg.

In his letter, George said, "The Yukon boys knew their jobs." They had had thorough training in machine gun tactics in England, but along with training they had "nerve and determination."[50] They were sometimes compared to the troops from Newfoundland, on the far side of Canada. Both had grown up in a harsh landscape, which made them tough and resilient, already seasoned to adversity.

It was generally agreed that the actions of the machine gunners at Amiens and Villers-Bretonneux kept the Allied line intact. But the Yukon Battery had been decimated. With only 10 men left, it joined George Black's 17th Machine Gun Company to become the 2nd Canadian Motor Machine Gun Brigade.

When George was moved to the Royal Free Hospital in London, Martha could visit him. A few weeks later, he was sent to the Convalescent Home at Matlocks Baths in Derbyshire, and by October he could walk quite well. This became holiday time for Martha and George. They motored out of London, enjoying the fresh air, the cottages and grand old houses, the scenic English countryside. They knew the war was coming to an end, and their spirits lifted, but there was still heaviness in their hearts until they could know their boys were safe.

On November 11, the war was over. *My loved ones are safe now*, Martha told herself. She watched in delight as the mood of the English people transformed from stoic endurance to spontaneous wild celebration. Church bells rang; sirens sounded. People sang and danced in the street and cheered as workmen removed shields from city lights that had kept London dark for four years. They played musical instruments, blew bugles, formed street bands, blew factory whistles. Children danced and shouted with excitement and newfound freedom.

Lyman, youngest member of the Yukon Machine Gun Battery, leads the armoured cars in the official victory entry into Mons, Belgium. Yukon Archives, George Black fonds 81_107_198.

Warren and Donald had both survived the war. Donald never did get overseas. His letters to her always said he expected to be sent any day, but instead he was moved from one camp to another as an aviation training instructor. George was declared well just about the time the war ended and was now ordered to Germany with the Army of Occupation to advise on legal matters. On Christmas Day, he rejoined his men. Left alone in London, Martha was cheered by a letter from Colonel Muerlong, O.C. Yukon Machine Gun Battery:

> *It may interest you to know that I have given Lyman command of the armoured cars in the official entry into Mons. I thought it*

might be of interest to Yukon to have the youngest member take part in such an historical event.[51]

For his bravery at Villers-Bretonneux, Lyman was awarded the Military Cross at Buckingham Palace. Relatives were invited to the grounds of the palace to witness the ceremony. Martha loved pomp and circumstance, and nothing could be better than a ceremony honouring her youngest son.

While Lyman disappeared inside the palace with the other soldiers, she and the other guests awaited the proceedings in a roped-off area of the garden. It was typical of Martha on any occasion to observe her surroundings in detail and comment on the beauty of the décor. But there was a lack of beauty here. A red-and-white canopy held up by rough wooden props was worn and shabby. Red carpets led to a platform and a very plain table with a velvet cushion. There were two gold-backed chairs. As she waited, Martha's mind redecorated and rearranged the scene to add elegance to the occasion "with very little expense or effort." No doubt she added flowers. She did, however, make excuses for the royal family, as they probably wanted to demonstrate economy in time of war.

Another ceremony that Martha attended with Lady Perley, wife of the Canadian Ambassador, was the presenting of Regimental Colours in April. On this occasion, Lyman was one of the standard bearers.

In the spring of 1918, the first wave of Spanish influenza had swept through the military camps and hospitals, taking advantage of crowded conditions, poor nutrition, poor hygiene and stress. And with half the British forces falling sick, the German army was suffering too. Disease has always plagued armies, sometimes proving as deadly as the enemies they fought. This first wave was less virulent than what was to come, so many soldiers had a mild case—they called it the three-day fever—

and recovered. Lyman was probably one of these. In the fall, a second, more deadly wave spread rapidly until most of the world was dealing with it. Martha said the death toll in London was alarming. At least 20 million people would die before it was over in 1920; some estimates said 50 million. Somehow the Black family, scattered as they were in London or France or Belgium or the United States or the far east, survived it.

In springtime, Martha was sent to France by the Overseas Club to visit communities and villages ravaged by the war. The Overseas Club was a charity supplying soldiers with gift parcels. Beginning in 1915, it asked school children to raise money to fill boxes with useful items, socks, chocolates and cigarettes to be sent at Christmas. As Martha administered the Yukon Comfort Fund, she worked with the Overseas Club to get the parcels arriving in London from Dawson City delivered to wherever the Yukon soldiers were.

Now she was to examine battlefields and ruins and rural landscapes and suggest ways to restore and rejuvenate and beautify them. What she had only imagined in her nightmares in London now stood before her eyes. She trudged over battlefields, over torn-up fields, past shelled houses, over rusty barbed wire, past dug-outs and trenches, and always, everywhere, crosses and patches of scarlet poppies and blue cornflowers, vivid against the white chalk of upturned earth.

She was back in England, writing her report in time for a garden party at Buckingham Palace given for 1000 people who had been "war workers." It was a beautiful day, one she would always remember. The lawns of the palace were edged with flowers at their summer best. Guests lined both sides of the garden path, and their majesties walked between the lines, greeting them. Queen Mary wore a beautiful blue embroidered dress and hat. King George stopped to question Martha about her lecture work.

Martha, talking to the queen's dresser, said how much she would like to see the interior of the palace. Miss Sibley suggested that the person who might be able to arrange this would be Joe Boyle. Within a few days came the message summoning her to view the palace. She arrived through the Privy Purse door as directed and was met by Miss Sibley and the housekeeper.

Martha missed nothing. Queen Mary's boudoir, with its French blue tapestry, the sweet peas in crystal bowls, the hydrangeas in jardinieres, the carnations on her writing desk. There were cabinets that blazed with jewels and mementos of her empire travels. In sitting rooms and drawing rooms, Martha admired Chippendale furniture, beautiful watercolours, cabinets with daggers, swords, crowns and bejewelled belts.

The tour ended with tea shared with Miss Sibley. As they ate brown bread, butter, strawberry jam and fruitcake in her sitting room overlooking the gardens, the king and his dog were having tea with his mother, Queen Alexandra, in the garden.

Lyman returned to Canada before George or Martha. After his work in Germany, George was called upon to defend British Columbia soldiers charged with mutiny when riots broke out at Kimmel Camp in Wales. Here, 15,000 troops had been kept in limbo, waiting to get home to Canada when ships were not available to transport them. Conditions were bad, with Spanish flu, half-rations, shortages of tobacco and of coal to heat their huts. The men worried that delays in getting home would ruin their chances for jobs in Canada. In the riots, five soldiers were killed and several more wounded. When the trial was over, the Canadian Military Court of Inquiry imposed sentences that George felt were too harsh: ten years' jail time for one man, five years for five others.

George returned home to Canada in July. From Vancouver, he continued to work on behalf of the Kimmel soldiers, appealing to both the prime minister and the minister of justice. As a result of legal review, all 21 sentences were greatly reduced and all but two soldiers were released by 1920.

It was the middle of August before Martha set sail on the S.S. *Melita*. From Quebec City, she headed to Los Angeles, where her 80-year-old father was ill. George Munger had always been there for Martha on every step of her adventures, never questioning her forays into the unexpected. He had lived long enough to see his daughter home from the war, and he knew that her husband and his grandsons, Warren, Donald, and Lyman, had survived. With Donald nearby, Martha now saw a lot of him. Sometimes they laughed over good times in Dawson City. Sometimes her father felt well enough to laugh with them. He died at the end of October. With a heavy heart, Martha said goodbye to her bereft mother and other family members and headed for Vancouver.

Canadians returning home after the war found that time had moved on without them. This was true for George and Martha. The position George gave up for war service, Commissioner of the Yukon, no longer existed. It had been merged with the office of Gold Commissioner. Yukon councilors were reduced to three, one each for Dawson, Whitehorse and Mayo. Their beautiful Government House was closed and shuttered.

The war had taken a big chunk out of their lives. Now feeling suddenly older, "tired and childless," they had to forge a new life. Lyman had chosen to remain in military service. George resumed his law practice in Vancouver. They bought a small cottage on the north shore of Burrard Inlet.

After a rainy Vancouver winter, spring arrived early. The soft sea air restored Martha, and she turned to gardening. Any time after 5 a.m., she could be seen at work among her flowers or raking seaweed on the beach for fertilizer while watching the ships move in and out of the harbour.

1921-1957
Yukon–Ottawa Years

TWO YEARS AFTER they settled in Vancouver, a federal election changed their lives again. In the fall of 1921, a delegation called on George to offer him the federal Conservative nomination for the Yukon.

George accepted and headed north for what Martha called the hardest political battle of his life.

It was certainly physically the hardest. With no radio coverage in the North, he could only reach his voters by going to them. When he arrived in Whitehorse too late for the river steamers, he paddled by canoe to Fort Selkirk, 160 miles (259 km), as slush ice formed on the river. From there he set out with a guide to snowshoe another 100 miles (160 km) up the frozen Stewart River to Mayo's mining community. Although gold had been discovered on Duncan Creek in the Mayo area in 1901, it was the 1919 discovery of silver-lead deposits on Keno Hill that had made Mayo and Keno an important mining area by 1921 and an essential part of George's campaign trail. From Mayo, he set out by dog team for Dawson.

George, at 48, is no longer the young man who climbed the White Pass. When he falls through the ice along the way, the soaking-freezing brings on pneumonia. When he is well enough to head for home, he leaves Dawson in an automobile. Near the North Fork, the car rolls over, pinning him underneath. His only good luck is that, once he is rescued, a trained nurse married to an engineer at North Fork power plant is available to help him. Bruised and battered, he has three broken ribs. When he sets out one more time, he is on a bed on a dogsled, pulled as carefully as possible to Whitehorse on the Overland Trail by Conservative supporters who know this man is their only hope to unseat the Liberal candidate, whom they claim is corrupt.

If anyone ever deserved to win an election by dint of hard work and determination to connect with his constituents at whatever cost, George Black did in 1921. And he won.

The living pattern of the Blacks now became nomadic: Ottawa when Parliament was is session, Dawson in the summer, and sometimes Vancouver in between. It was a different Dawson after the war. Most of the men who had gone off with Joe Boyle's Machine Gun Company or George Black's Infantry Company did not come back. Of Boyle's 50, only 10 men survived. Most of the Yukon soldiers who did return to Canada looked for work elsewhere. Dawson's heyday was over.

George and Martha had both known Dawson when the population shifted and swirled between 20,000 and 30,000. They had seen it settle down but contain enough graft and corruption to support a whole host of lawyers. Now, in the '20s, it was a quieter and mostly law-abiding place. While George still practiced law in the summers, the legislation he steered through Parliament decreased crime in the goldfields and shrunk his own living.

They were caught in Dawson one time when a telegram summoned George back to Ottawa by December 10. To make the 4000-mile (6440 km) journey, they would have to catch the *Princess Louise* in Skagway eight days later. First, they had to reach the railhead at Whitehorse, 332 miles (435 km) away. They started out in a Model T racing car,

Heading south in a Model T. in December, to catch the sleigh at the first road house on the start of their 4000-mi (6500-km) journey to Ottawa. MacBride Museum of Yukon History, 1933_29_62.

hoping to catch the stage that had departed Dawson that morning and could be overtaken at its first roadhouse. Martha would remember this trip as a "glorious winter trip out."

> It was a clear, cold aurora night, with gorgeous prism-coloured northern lights flaming and dancing across the heavens." They left at 11 p.m. and did not reach the roadhouse until 3 a.m. They were on the stage at 7 next morning. Low in spirits from lack of sleep, travel-sore and hungry, they reached a large roadhouse that night. Martha could recall the dinner years later: "Creamy barley soup, tender delicious moose steak and roast wild ducks, native cranberry jelly, celery and head lettuce, biscuits and cheese.[52]

They drove next morning over flats where poplar trees were covered in frost, branches and twigs sparkling like jewels and cobwebs catching the sun like silver lace. At the Stewart River, the ice was not yet safe for the stage, so passengers walked across, fearing the alarming sounds the ice was making. Horses were taken across one by one, while the mail and luggage was pulled over on hand-sleds.

In Ottawa, George was drafting legislation to make life better for miners and other Yukon workers. By this time, the corruption rife in Yukon could be found in Ottawa as well. Corporations with big pockets would lobby and bribe officials to acquire large tracts for hydraulic and dredging rights, ignoring the rights of small-time miners. George's Yukon Quartz Mining Act of 1924 rewrote Canadian mining law to provide legal security of tenure to mining claims and end bureaucratic interference.

George won three more elections, in 1925, 1926 and 1930, always working in Parliament to give the Yukon more security and stability. He secured for Yukon people the same rights to jury trial as in the rest of the country. He advised the government on a system of fair taxation on lode mining profits, to protect the economic future of the mining industry. He also worked on a committee dealing with pensions and soldiers' affairs.

In 1930, under R.B. Bennett, George was elected Speaker of the House, or "First Commoner." Pierre Berton, son of Laura and Frank, recalled his father taking him to Ottawa to see Parliament when he was 11. This future writer of popular Canadian history missed nothing, but what he remembered with the most glee was that, when the dignitaries filed past him, the Speaker of the House actually winked at him. George Black had recognized the boy from Dawson City.

George's position made him official host of the House of Commons and put Martha in her element. Once again, she was "hostess of

Government House," presiding over dinner parties at the Chateau Laurier, arranging entertainment for visiting dignitaries, choosing linens, china, glass and silver, planning refreshments and decorations, arranging flowers. Martha was a connoisseur of fashion and ceremony. Her eye for detail and knowledge of styles and fabrics and etiquette leaves us vivid pictures of decades more gracious than the present. She describes the opening ceremony of the 17th session of Parliament.

> *We stood as the vice-regal party entered the Red Chamber, and His Majesty's representative took his seat on the dais under the red canopy. Following him, Her Excellency, looking very queenly, wearing a coronet of diamonds and a handsome black gown, with court train, silver-embroidered in a Greek-key pattern, borne by two pages, took her seat to the left. I see again the Prime Minister, Mr. Bennett to the right, in Windsor uniform of gold-braided coat, white satin breeches, buckled shoes, and long stockings; the brilliantly coloured uniforms of military officers; the red woolsack, on which sat the Chief Justice and Supreme Court Judges in their scarlet and ermine robes and cocked hats; the Sergeant-at-arms carrying the mace, the massive gold staff surmounted by the crown; the Gentleman Usher of the Black Rod, and His Excellency, bowing in formal procedure; the diplomatic corps, representing many nations; the galaxy of beautiful women in gorgeous gowns contrasting with the formal black and white of the senators and unders.*[53]

Martha said a lady's formal court dress was an evening gown of any colour with a long train, tulle veil with white feathers and long white gloves. At the reception that evening that she and George hosted at the Chateau Laurier, she remembers that the ladies' gowns were mostly

"Tory blue." After nine years of Liberal government, the Conservative ladies were expressing themselves in colour.

Wherever Martha went, she had connections. It was easy to converse with guests she had met previously in London or Vancouver or Dawson City. Lady Perley, as wife of the High Commissioner to Britain, had driven Martha out to Seaford at the end of the war for the presenting of Regimental Colours. Lord and Lady Byng had visited the Yukon in 1922, when he was Governor General. Martha and Lady Byng had hiked the hills together looking for rare wild flowers. Martha had a unique ability to find common ground with anyone she met, whether she was being presented to King George V in London or making sandwiches for a robber fugitive in Dawson.

She recalled a dinner with their excellencies Lord and Lady Bessborough in attendance, Lady Bessborough a radiant beauty in silver and blue mistral. Martha wore pale blue crepe banded with mink. The tables for 40 guests were laid with blue linen and decorated with forget-me-nots and talisman roses. Martha took her hostess duties seriously. When George asked her at 11 p.m. one night to arrange a luncheon next day for the Spanish ambassador, she worked on the guest list until 2 a.m.

In 1931, she was asked to be national president of the IODE but decided to turn it down. Her life was busy enough, always on the move from Ottawa to Vancouver to Dawson, 4000 miles in all. What she and George needed was a holiday. In 1932, they treated themselves to a European vacation, which included tea at No. 10 Downing Street as well as high tea and a visit with Her Royal Highness the Duchess of York (wife of the future King George VI).

OPPOSITE: *As the wife of the first Commoner (Speaker of the House), Martha was hostess at official occasions, planning, decorating and entertaining guests, a role that suited her perfectly. Yukon Archives, Munger family fonds, 78_112_ 4.*

The 1930s were not easy years for the country, or for the Blacks. As the Great Depression tightened its hold, it caught George in its grip. In 1935, he had a nervous breakdown caused by "financial and personal" troubles. He resigned as Speaker in January 1935. The details of his depression are not spelled out. Financial losses must have played a big part, as they did for so many in the 1930s. His law practice had been disrupted by war and politics. His salary as an MP was not large enough to compensate for on-again off-again law practice and their travel expenses. The Blacks may have been wealthy for a while, but they had lived generously; Conservative in politics, they were liberal in their lifestyle.

If there were more personal aspects, these are carefully avoided in Martha's correspondence and biography. There is never mention of trouble in their marriage, although it may not always have been easy for George to be Martha's husband. She had a way of focusing all the energy in a room, and George, a quieter, more serious person, must have sometimes stood in her shadow.

That George was admitted to a veterans' hospital suggests that he suffered from war trauma, an affliction which we would now call PTSD (post-traumatic stress disorder). He had seen Yukon men fall in battle. One of them that he remembered was Charlie O'Brien, a young schoolboy of Lyman's age. Another was Angus McKellar, of the North West Mounted Police. In a letter to Martha during the war he had described "wallowing in earth churned up with blood," as he moved his men past dead bodies, with the noise of big guns and the rattle of machine guns, and the groans of wounded and dying men.

Did his trauma also go back to the Whitehorse Trail and Dead Horse Pass in 1898? George's party managed to get their horses to the top in good enough condition to sell them (one of his party was an experienced teamster) but he witnessed scenes of desperation and animal cruelty among men unprepared and unfit for the trail.

Physically, too, George was battered and scarred. His appendicitis operation had serious complications. He was wounded in the war. Then he had suffered pneumonia, broken ribs and possible internal injuries on the campaign trail.

Lyman came to the aid of his parents. A distraught wife and a son whom Martha described as "a tower of strength" got George into Westminster Hospital in London, Ontario. This was a veterans' hospital opened in 1920 for the treatment and rehabilitation of soldiers with psychological problems and shell shock suffered in the war. After 1929, it expanded to include general medical and surgical treatment. With 400 acres, the hospital used nature as a healing tool; its peaceful setting let veterans fish in Walker Pond and engage in healthful sports. George was there for six months. When he was released in July, Martha took him to the Yukon, believing that the Yukon's power to heal and restore were what he needed most.

George was not the only Conservative in trouble that year. Prime Minister R.B. Bennett had been navigating the worst economic times in the history of Canada. An election was called for October, and a desperate electorate was looking for any alternative that might better their lives. Bennett had held on to his platform of free enterprise until 1935, when he changed course, emulating Roosevelt's New Deal south of the border. Bennett's new deal now promised minimum wages, unemployment insurance, old-age pensions and taxation reform. But it came too late. A bachelor prime minister living in style in the Chateau Laurier seemed to have no connection to the lives of ordinary Canadians as they battled unemployment and crop failures and drove their Bennett Buggies (automobiles pulled by horses because owners could not afford gasoline).

George Black was not well enough to fight an election. Martha was asked to run in his place as an Independent Conservative, meaning a political Conservative who lacked a formal affiliation to the party. Martha turned to her father for advice. He said, "Daughter, you have the gift of gab. You might possibly succeed. Do the men up there like you?"

"Some do and some don't."

Her father said, "We never had any he-women [suffragettes] in our family, but if you take it, you get it."[54]

There was a Yukon joke that said the territory had only two parties—the Liberals and the Blacks. The Blacks were a team; if George was out of the running, that left Martha to carry on.

There were still no radio stations covering the vast territory of Yukon. Again, as in 1921, the only way to reach a voter was to go find him. This she did by steamer, motorboat, plane, car, teams of horses and on foot. When her car got mired in mud, she walked two miles for help. Once she walked several miles to contact three voters, who would have to walk eight miles to vote. (She heard that they did vote for her.) When her motorboat often left her stranded on a wild shore, she encountered caribou, ptarmigan, and once, a bear cub. "But often in the rugged beauty and quiet of that wonderful country, I forgot all about politics and searched for wild flowers."[55] Martha would always respond to the spell of the Yukon that Robert Service described so perfectly.

> *It's the beauty that thrills me with wonder,*
> *It's the stillness that fills me with peace.*[56]

There were hecklers and naysayers, people who doubted "this old woman" could help their "down and out" situations, others who said she was running a sob-sister campaign. These were hurtful remarks, but George was ill and she had to stand in his place. She told herself to "mush on," remembering Service's Law of the Yukon:

> "Send not your foolish and feeble;
> send me your strong and your sane." [57]

All across Canada, Conservative voters turned Liberal, and the country swept William Lyon Mackenzie King into Parliament with the largest majority ever in Canada: 171 seats for the Liberals to 39 for the Conservatives. But the Independent Conservative in the Yukon won her seat.

On her way to Ottawa, Martha visited Lyman and his wife, Aimee, in Winnipeg and laughed as Lyman told her about election night. With friends, he and Aimee had gathered around the radio. They had listened as the sweeping Liberal win came in but had heard no results for the Yukon. Late at night they turned off the radio, and Lyman said, "Well, I guess poor old Mother is another also-ran."

Next morning, Lyman phoned the *Winnipeg Free Press* to ask, "Who got in in Yukon?"

The question was passed around, and the answer came back, "Oh, that other dame!"[58]

The "other dame" proceeded to Ottawa and the opening of the 18th session of Parliament, February 6, 1936. As she took her seat and watched the Commons elect a Speaker, her heart went out to George, left behind in Vancouver. She was not happy taking his place. Although she had opinions on everything, she did not see herself as a politician.

From today's perspective on gender equality, Martha's attitude seems surprising, even quaint. She never hesitated to march into a man's world when it suited her—climb the Chilkoot, mine for gold with 16 men, run a sawmill, ride a hand-car and freight train in the Rockies or a troopship filled with soldiers—but she did not want to take George's place. There is sometimes a faint echo of her mother defending her father's insensitivity when his twins were born—"Not a man like your dear father." There was a glass ceiling she did not care to break.

She had been happy as the chatelaine, the gracious hostess, a role she performed with ease. In her biography she says, "I was never happier than at the time of the 1930 opening, when he was elected Speaker. I enjoyed all the attendant personal honours, as wife of the First Commoner." Now, at the age of 70, she was here alone. "I look at the Speaker's empty chair, and my eyes fill with tears."[59]

There was a general atmosphere of gloom over the opening of Parliament in 1936: black armbands on military officers, black gowns and gloves on the women. King George V had died on January 20. Edward VIII was now king. Prime Minister William Lyon Mackenzie King, as well as Opposition leader R.B. Bennett, voiced their sympathy to the royal family. As Martha listened, her thoughts were with Queen Mary and pleasant memories of her during the war. She passed a note to A.C. Casselman, Conservative party whip, asking if she should extend to Queen Mary the sympathy of the women of Canada. He answered, "I think not."

Martha, being Martha, ignored him; she rose for the first time in Parliament, fearing her voice would fail her, and eloquently offered a tribute of regret and sympathy to Queen Mary. She had expressed her sincere feelings, but she had also let it be known that she was not just a pleasant face filling an empty chair.

In these years, she was in great demand as a public speaker, and she could never turn down an invitation to speak about her Yukon. She was also writing about the Yukon for magazines like *Chatelaine*, *The*

In 1933, Canadian Geographical Journal published Martha's "Yukon Wild Flowers." Its first page featured the purple pasque flower or crocus (Anemone nutalliana), Martha's favourite. It became the Yukon's floral emblem during her lifetime. Photo: Enid Mallory.

Province, *The Canadian Home Journal* or the *I.O.D. Echoes*. In 1933, *Canadian Geographic* published her article "Yukon and Her Flowers." In 1940, Price Templeton published it as *Yukon Wild Flowers*, a 95-page pamphlet. Its first page featured the purple pasque flower (Anemone nutalliana), Martha's favourite. She described it as a crocus, like the garden variety but with soft hairy down to protect it from harsh weather. She considered it pretty even after it bloomed, when the long, silky tails of its seeds formed a lovely feathery tuft.

Another 38-page pamphlet, *Klondike Days*, was published by Acme Press. In a pamphlet called *Memories of a Yukon Summer*, she and

George published 19 photos of Yukon flowers as "a reminder that Yukon has floral beauties quite as interesting as her golden output and her winter snow and ice." The photos were black and white, but Martha's words painted them in evocative colours for anyone who had wandered Yukon hills. "Arnica: Bright yellow flowers with a pungent odor. Indian macerate: the roots used for bruises. Mountain phlox: Very lovely pink flowers. On high hills during June and early July. And one of her favourites, the Siberian, or Franklin, lady's slipper: The sac white with overhanging caps of green and two wings pure white."[60]

She was also working on her autobiography with co-author Elizabeth Bailey Price, but in February 1937 McClelland & Stewart changed their mind about publishing it, a great disappointment to Martha. [Thomas Nelson would publish it a year later as *My Seventy Years*.]

The late '30s were to be Martha's hardest years. The Great Depression, George's personal depression, her biography turned down, then tragedy! On February 27, 1937, her son Lyman was travelling from Kingston to Ottawa with an army friend. His wife, Aimee, was in Ottawa staying with Martha, both of them looking forward to Lyman's arrival. Lyman never arrived. He was killed in an automobile accident on Highway 16.

Martha was heartbroken. She had to stay strong to help Aimee, her young daughter-in-law, who had lost her love and her future dreams. But in her diary, Martha said, "I feel bowed and broken for the first time in my life."[61] Lyman was her Yukon son, the happy baby that had turned despair to delight in the winter of 1899, the war hero and the son who had helped them through George's darkest days. Now, just turned 38, he was gone.

Martha carried on, trying to help Aimee, trying to lose her own grief in work. March 15: "At the House. Carried on as usual. Some days I feel fresh and able to go on—on others it is with great difficulty that I can whip myself up to take any interest in people or my work but that will never do. Again, on March 17: "I seem to have lost my grip. I am tired when I get up, tired when I go to bed—tired in mind and body."[62]

Martha also feared what this would do to George, still recovering, still trying to re-establish his law practice in Vancouver. He had now lost his only son, the little boy who latched on to his stepfather's name the minute he married Martha.

When Parliament prorogued, the Blacks headed north to find solace in Yukon's grandeur, warmth in its midnight sun. But there was more bad news to come. In August they had word that Martha's eldest son, Warren, had died in Honolulu, Hawaii. He was 48. Warren, under Father Purdy's care, had been educated at Notre Dame, then at the Naval Academy at Annapolis, Maryland, and had served in the war in the Pacific. After the war, he worked for the Black Diamond Steamship Lines, travelling from New York to Rotterdam, Holland, as well as to British ports. Because of a heart condition, he had moved to Hawaii and served on a cruiser in inland ports. His father, Will Purdy, had died in Hawaii in 1930. Warren had had more contact with his father than Donald because his teenage years were spent in Grandfather Purdy's care. Along with his wife, he left behind two daughters and a son, Martha's faraway grandchildren.

Martha was back in Ottawa by January 1936 and had Aimee living with her at 251 Cooper Street. On the first of February, she got news that George Munger had died the day before in the State Tuberculosis Hospital in Salem, Oregon. This was the brother who had let her join the gold rush stampede without Will, who helped her over the summit and supported her as she struggled with her fears before Lyman was born. The claims he staked had paid off at first, but like many others, he found there were better ways to survive in Dawson than digging gold. Joe Boyle saw that Dawson needed a laundry, and George, experienced in his father's laundry empire, managed the Boyle steam laundry. When he left the Yukon, he worked in the laundry business for many years. His wife also died in 1938, leaving behind two sons, Lyman and Paul.

Martha's only brother was gone, along with two of her sons. Only Donald remained. She found herself thinking often of the eight-year-old who had stood staunchly beside her when her sawmill crew deserted her. Donald had received excellent schooling in Dawson, where high wages and adventure attracted good teachers. He then went to Los Angeles to attend Stanford University under the watchful eyes of his Munger grandparents, who had retired there. He graduated a mechanical engineer. In the war he served as a second lieutenant, training airmen. Before the beginning of the Second World War, he was president of the Curran Lumber Company; his early training at his mother's sawmill in Dawson not gone to waste. When he left to join the war, he was commissioned a captain in the U.S. army and became a technical executive officer in the air corps.

During Martha's time in Parliament, there were proposals for a joint U.S.-Canada highway from the contiguous United States to Alaska, but the two countries could not agree on who should pay what share of it. Martha and George, who had travelled so often by rail, steamer and stage, were keen campaigners for a highway. George never forgot that first trip by automobile just before New Year's, 1913, his calculated effort to convince Parliament that such a road could be travelled even in a Yukon winter.

In an interview for the *Alaska Weekly* in March 1940, Martha was asked about her hopes for the road and said, "It will be built when both Canada and the United States want it badly enough."[63] The Second World War gave them both the reason to want it badly enough. The

United States feared a Japanese attack on Alaska. It was agreed that Canada would provide the corridor and the U.S. would bear the full cost. After the war, the U.S. would turn the road over to Canada. President Franklin D. Roosevelt got approval for the project in February, and construction began on March 8, 1942.

The little town of Whitehorse became a bustling construction city and transportation hub as heavy equipment arrived by train and went to work on the road in both directions. The Alaska Highway became a feat of modern engineering, as 10,000 workers pushed it through rock and forest wilderness and over five mountain ranges. It began at the railhead in Dawson Creek, British Columbia, and stretched 2451 km to Delta Junction, Alaska. By 1944, it was a passable but very rough road, not opened to the public until 1947.

It was disappointing to Martha and George that the route chosen did not go through Dawson. Instead, it veered west, just north of Whitehorse, to go through Haines Junction, then northwest, crossing into Alaska at Beaver Creek, then on to meet Alaska's Richardson Highway at Delta Junction. Their dream of a road from Whitehorse to Dawson would have to wait for the Klondike Highway, which would run from Skagway, Alaska, to Dawson City, Yukon, along the route of the gold-seekers in 1898. From Whitehorse, the North Klondike portion would follow a piece of the Alaska Highway, then head north to Dawson 323 miles (520 km). For a time, it ran north to Stewart Crossing, then veered east to Mayo and Keno's silver mines before reaching Dawson. When it finally opened in 1955, it ended the era of steamboat travel on the Yukon River.

George was well enough to run in the 1940 election, so Martha stepped aside. He won and took his seat in Parliament. He was successful again in 1945, but in 1949, when Yukon was merged with the Northwest Territory, he chose not to run. When the two territories were separated again for the 1953 election, he did run—but for the first time was defeated.

In 1944, George and Martha bought a home in Whitehorse that overlooked the Yukon River. George's law practice in Dawson had declined as Dawson itself declined. From a city of 30,000, it had dwindled to less than 1,000 after the war. There was a deserted air to Dawson now—buildings shuttered, tilted or falling. For those who had been there in its glory days, it was hard to see.

In the 1940s and '50s, accidents plagued Martha. A fire in her toaster set the curtains above it on fire, and Martha was burned fighting the flames. While she healed in the nearby Regina Hotel, her house was repaired. She got a new kitchen, and George got a new office wing.

Then a broken hip put her in a wheelchair. It was hard not to be able to garden anymore or look for wildflowers in the spring. She could still shut her eyes and be back on a Yukon creek, carrying a gun or a camera, but her legs would no longer take her there. She kept up a lively social life from her wheelchair, and correspondence with old friends brightened her days.

In March 1949 Martha was made an Officer of the Order of the British Empire, acknowledging her cultural and social contributions to the Yukon. She was unable to go to Ottawa to receive the award. Instead, the Governor General came to Victoria, where she had spent a month in hospital and was now recovering at the Prior Guest House.

George, busy in Vancouver, was unable to attend, but Martha wrote him a long letter describing the ceremony at Government House in Victoria and telling him how nervous she was. But she did still manage a flawless curtsy, after which came a delicious cocktail, "and did I need it." Her letter said she was looking forward to George's arrival after Easter Sunday and hoped he would stay for some time.

Soon after, George was honoured by being appointed to the Privy Council, its purpose being to provide nonpartisan advice and support, leadership and coordination to the Governor General. As well, he still had his Vancouver law practice, which he did not give up until 1956.

In 1953, the Yukon capital was transferred from Dawson City to Whitehorse. Whitehorse was the transportation hub for the territory, with railroad and river traffic and now the highway. The highway that Martha and George had long campaigned for had shunned Dawson and made Whitehorse the centre of the territory.

When she was 89, they flew to Dawson City for Discovery Days. They were able to stay in Government House, now being used by St. Mary's Hospital as a home for the aged. It was wonderful to sleep in her Government House again, but it was also upsetting. Interviewed afterward by Flo Whyard, she said, "Dawson is a wreck!" She was saddened to see the buildings leaning to the left or the right or backward. "People have left Dawson. I saw three of my old homes down there, and they made my heart sick."[64] Martha would not live long enough to see Dawson restored and revitalized. Parks Canada would not start to work on the town until the 1970s.

Dawson was now a tired little town that had once been a great city, its population greater than Winnipeg's, a rich, exciting place where you wanted to be. You did not have to dig gold to get rich in Dawson. You could practice law, run a sawmill, build a dance hall or laundry, sell newspapers, import anything and sell it at a grand profit. And you were having a grand time. It took a while to realize that your city had dwindled and you were no longer rich and you should go.

Most of those who had followed the Trail of '98 over the mountains went home as soon as they realized there was no gold for them. But thousands stayed because the Yukon had got a hold of them. For some, it was the mystic love of the gold itself that would not let go. There were young men who stayed on the creeks looking for that gold until they were old men. For others, like George and Martha, it was the land, the light, the air, the flowers, the wildlife, the elusive quality that was Yukon. It was simply where they belonged, and they knew it from the start. Anywhere else had to be compared to the Yukon, and the Yukon always won.

Most who went north for gold did not die rich. Those who found the gold had a wild time for a while, but the gold dust slipped through their fingers in the dance halls and saloons; they lost it to dance-hall queens or poker games. When it was gone, they headed outside to look for an ordinary job and a wife. Some of them could not adjust to ordinary life and drank themselves to death.

What they had given up to their Yukon years could never be measured, but most of them would do it again, given the chance. Exhausted, at the top of the Chilkoot, Martha had said to herself, "I would never do it again, knowing now what it meant … Not for all the gold in the Klondyke." But later, looking back, she asked herself, "knowing now what it meant, would I miss it? … No, never! … Not even for all the gold in the world!"[65]

Martha embraced the world as she found it—rose to its challenges and did what she could to make the lives around her better. She brought a bit of home to lonesome miners; she supported George in his work to improve the lives of boat crews, loggers and miners. She worked tirelessly in London to comfort soldiers caught up in the Great War. She made Yukoners proud of their Dawson City and its beautiful Government House. She added elegance to Canada's Parliament.

She shared her love and joy of the Yukon while carting her glass slides around England and North America. Her study of Yukon wild flowers, her displays in CPR grand hotels, the interest she and George took in birds and wild animals, all contributed to early conservation movements. Later in life, they were writing letters expressing concern about wildlife areas being taken over by military groups. Through Martha's autobiography and magazine writings, people saw the land as she and George saw it when they, "tramped the Yukon trails and paddled the Yukon streams, he with a camera slung over his shoulder." By this time, George had given up hunting and concentrated on his photography.

Their explorations were not limited to the Dawson vicinity. Martha knew the coast of Alaska as well as the hills of Yukon and the Ogilvie Mountains, the Arctic poppies and wild roses at Carcross, the chocolate lilies at Skagway and the blue iris at Dyea, On the high hills between Keno and Wernecke, she walked among blue mountain forget-me-nots, pink snakeweed and cerise shooting star. She was delighted to find, along the road from Juneau to the Mendenhall glacier, 15 miles of blue lupines. Beneath the glacier, she found acres of silvery cotton grass, as well as the rarer golden-beige variety. Her *Yukon Wild Flowers* published as a pamphlet in 1940, was the first published record of Yukon flora. Her artistic displays mimicked the kaleidoscope of colour on the hills in spring or the woven mats of red and gold spread out on purple-white mountains in fall.

In the 1950s, Martha campaigned for the pasque flower or crocus (Anemone nutalliana), to become the floral emblem of the Yukon Terrirory. This little purple-blue flower poked its head through the Yukon snow each spring, covered in soft hairy down to keep it warm. What she wanted was causing a problem because it had been Manitoba's provincial flower for some time. It was a measure of the Territorial Council's respect for Martha that they named the pasque flower the Yukon emblem anyway. They would change it to the fireweed (Epilobium angustifolium) after Martha's death. Meanwhile, her writing and public speaking, along with George's photography, like the poems of Robert

Yukon-Ottawa Years

Service, were putting the Yukon on everyone's map and making it a last-frontier tourist destination.

Martha was now considered a celebrity and an attraction to visiting dignitaries. Among her callers was the Duke of Edinburgh, on his solo tour that the press dubbed his "stag party." After opening the British Empire and Commonwealth Games in Vancouver, he arrived in Whitehorse, where he visited Martha. Another caller was Governor General Vincent Massey. When he referred to her time in the Yukon and her marriage of almost 60 years, she replied, "It's been a hell of a long time!"[66] Protocol and deportment were very important to Martha; she knew exactly how to behave with royalty or any distinguished guest, but sometimes she just let it all slip and spoke like a seasoned prospector just in from the creeks.

Each year, a Sourdough Convention was held somewhere on the West Coast. Most of those who had whooped it up in the glory days of Yukon were retired in Vancouver or Victoria or in sunny California. They got together to reminisce, relive, and laugh about the times they had when they were young in Dawson City or Mayo or Whitehorse, and they recited the poetry of Robert Service. Service had attended his last convention in 1948, but each year he sent a poem. The 1955 convention was held in Eureka, California. The Blacks were unable to attend, but Martha sent the recipe for her famed Sourdough pancakes, which she first made on the shore of Lake Lindeman. In 1956, when Martha was 89, she and George flew to Vancouver and stayed at the Devonshire hotel, where the convention was held. George, at 83, was guest speaker at the convention.

|| OPPOSITE: *Prince Philip, Duke of Edinburgh, visits Martha during his 1954 Canadian tour. McBride Museum of Yukon History, 1989_26_333.*

A month later, Martha entertained 100 guests for her 90th birthday. To the *Whitehorse Star*, she said there were troubles that seemed unbearable at the time, but now in her memories there were only happy days.

Flo Whyard interviewed her for her 90th birthday. Listening to it today, one hears a voice that is strong, her manner of speaking reflecting her long-ago training in elocution at St. Mary's of Notre Dame. She talks about the terrible climb over the Chilkoot, the birth of Lyman, the kindness of George to her sons, the wonderful days at Government House, her love of the land. At the end of the interview, she says that all she does now is sit and think. "I realize now I should have done a great deal more."[67] At the age of 90, Martha is feeling the need of another challenge, her ambition still there while her body is wearing out.

Martha died on October 31, 1957. She was 91.

Outside newspapers said that all Canada looked to the Yukon with a bow when Martha Black died. the *Whitehorse Star's* front page read:

> *A blithe spirit has left the Yukon. Martha Louise Black was the unrivaled queen of all that host of men and women who sought the northern magic … she, above all, caught and reflected the true spirit of the Yukon, and some of it died with her.*[68]

It had been a long journey from the 1860s to the 1950s, from Chicago and the great fire to the Klondike Gold Rush, to her Rocky Mountain exploration, to wartime London and the Parliament of Canada. At her parents' beautiful ranch in Kansas, she had fallen into depression, but she knew what she needed. "What I wanted was not shelter and safety, but liberty and opportunity." That was what the

Yukon offered; that was what she grasped. And it had all been one great adventure.

At her funeral, two flags covered her coffin: the Canadian Red Ensign and the American Stars and Stripes. Martha was Canadian to the core, a Conservative, Anglican and Imperialist. But she was also American, and she saw no problem being both. It was by her request that her coffin was draped with the two flags, her final chance to express her love of ceremony and décor.

Shortly after Martha's funeral, a woman named Sadie King arrived to help George sort and pack up the house. She was the widow of a Vancouver builder and a close friend of George. They were married soon after in Vancouver. George, six years younger than Martha, was 85 and lived until he was 92.

Just how close George and Sadie were, and for how long, is an unanswered question. Perhaps it does not matter. Whatever distractions George and Martha had along the way, they remained a team, proud of each other, ready to campaign, defend, and if necessary, cover for each other.

After her death, Martha continued to be honoured by Canadians. In 1980, the highest peak in the Auriol Range of the Elias Mountains was officially named Mount Martha Black. On a good day it can be seen from the Alaska Highway 7 miles (11 km) southwest of Haines Junction. Another peak in the Big Salmon Range was named Mount Black for George, who had staked and worked his claim there on Livingstone Creek. A Canadian Coast Guard vessel built in Vancouver in 1986 was named the *Martha L. Black*. In 1997, Martha was featured on a Canada Post stamp. Black Street in Whitehorse is named for the couple who were often called Mr. and Mrs. Yukon. In August 2018, a bust of Martha was unveiled in Whitehorse, at the corner of Main Street and Fourth Ave.

What would have pleased her most would be seeing her beloved Government House restored to the happy years when she and George and their boys were there. Work began on the house in the 1970s, and when it was opened to the public the columns gleamed white again against the golden yellow of the house.

Inside, the spacious entrance hall is adorned with big-game mounted heads. The chandelier lights up the golden tones of the wallpaper. The beautiful staircase has been restored to polished beauty, the paneling buffed, the mahogany furniture tastefully arranged in the drawing, living and dining rooms, the silver and china on display. And there are flowers in every room.

Her spirit is still there. The visitors who enter may feel Martha Black drawing them in, the welcome gracious and all-inclusive.

Bibliography

Books

Becker, Ethel Anderson, *Klondike '98 (Hegg's Album of the 1898 Alaska Gold Rush)*. Portland, Oregon: Binfords & Mort, 1958.

Berton, Laura Beatrice. *I Married the Klondike*. Toronto: McClelland and Stewart, 1967.

Berton, Pierre. *The Klondike Fever: The Life and Death of the Last Great Gold Rush*. New York: Alfred A Knopf, 1958.

Black, Mrs. George, *My Seventy Years: As told to Elizabeth Baily Price*. Toronto: Thomas Nelson and Sons, 1938.

Bolotin, Norman, *A Klondike Scrapbook: Ordinary People, Extraordinary Times*. San Francisco: Chronicle Books, 1987.

Carpenter, Frank G., *Carpenter's World Travels: Canada and Newfoundland*. Garden City, N.Y.: Doubleday, Page & Company, 1924.

Coates, Ken S. & William R. Morrison. *Land of the Midnight Sun: A History of the Yukon*. Edmonton: Hurtig Publishers, 1988.

Frisch, Robert, *Birds by the Dempster Highway*. Victoria: Morriss Printing Company, 1999.

Gates, Michael, *From the Klondike to Berlin: The Yukon in World War I*: Vancouver: Lost Moose (Harbour Publishing) 2017.

Mallory, Enid, *Robert Service Under the Spell of the Yukon*. Victoria: Heritage House, 2006.

Martin, Carol, *Gold Rush Pioneer,* Vancouver: Douglas & McIntyre, 1966.

Wilson, Graham, *The Klondike Gold Rush: Photographs from 1896-1899*. Whitehorse: Wolf Creek Books, 1997.

Whyard, Flo, *Martha Black (Formerly My Ninety Years)*, Anchorage: Alaska Northwest Books, 1989.

Newspapers, Periodicals, Archival Sources

Canadian Geographical Journal
Canadian Historic Sites: Occasional Papers, Parks Canada
Chicago Daily Tribune
Dawson Daily News
Explore North
Gold Rush Diary of James McRae, Yukon Archives
"Kid in the Klondike" by Bert Parker
Los Angeles Herald
The Northern Review, Yukon College, Whitehorse
Yukon News

Endnotes

Over The Chilkoot

1. Flo Whyard, Interview for CBC, 1956.
2. Mrs. George Black, *My Seventy Years*, As told to Elizabeth Baily Price. Toronto: Thomas Nelson and Sons, 1938, 107.
3. Ibid. 68.
4. Ibid, 90.
5. Ibid, 17.
6. Ibid, 92.
7. Ibid, 93.
8. Ibid, 113
9. Ibid, 119.
10. Ibid, 128.
11. Ibid 23.
12. Ibid 126.
13. Ibid, 131.

Dawson High Society

14. Mrs. George Black, *My Seventy Years*, page 154.
15. Ibid, 156.
16. Ibid, 159.
17. Ibid, 162.
18. Flo Whyard (editor) *Martha Black* (Formerly *My Ninety Years*), Anchorage: Alaska Northwest Books, 1989, 160.

19 Gold Rush Diary of James McRae, Guelph, Ontario, February 1898 to January 20, 1901, Yukon Archives 80/1 F-101
20 Mrs. George Black, *My Seventy Years*, 184.
21 Ibid, 86.
22 Ibid, 167.
23 Ibid, 168.

First Lady Of The Yukon

24 Mrs. George Black, *My Seventy Years*, 205.
25 Ibid, 204.
26 Bert Parker, "Kid in the Klondike", 14.
27 Mrs. George Black, *My Seventy Years*, 217.
28 Ibid, page 219.
29 Eudora Ferry, *Klondike Sun*, July 8, 1993, 30.
30 Mrs. George Black, *My Seventy Years*, 222.
31 Frank G. Carpenter, *Carpenter's World Travels: Canada and Newfoundland*. Garden City, N.Y.: Doubleday, Page & Company, 1924, "By Motor Car Through the Wilderness", 239.
32 Mrs. George Black, *My Seventy Years*, 226.
33 Ibid, 228.

Mother To Yukon Soldiers

34 *Dawson Daily News*, July 3, 1916, 4
35 Mrs. George Black, *My Seventy Years*, 232
36 Ibid, 233.
37 Ibid, 235.
38 Ibid, 239
39 Ibid, 244
40 Ibid, 270
41 Ibid, 254.
42 Ibid, 256-57.

43 *Dawson Daily News*, August 20, 1917, 1.
44 *Dawson Daily News*, August 27, 1917, 4.
45 Mrs. George Black, *My Seventy Years*, 251.
46 Ibid, 246.
47 Letter from George Black to Martha, April 22, 1918, Yukon Archives, Martha Louise Black fonds, COR 249F15
48 Mrs. George Black, *My Seventy Years*, 247.
49 Ibid, 278.
50 Ibid, 278-80.
51 Ibid, 282

Yukon – Ottawa Years

52 Mrs. George Black, *My Seventy Years*, 290-291.
53 Ibid, 296.
54 Flo Whyard, Interview for CBC, 1956.
55 Mrs. George Black, *My Seventy Years*, 310.
56 Robert Service, *Songs of a Sourdough*, Toronto: William Briggs, 1909, 24.
57 Ibid, 11.
58 Mrs. George Black, *My Seventy Years*, 311.
59 Ibid, 312.
60 George and Martha Louise Black, "Memories of a Yukon Summer", ca 1938.
61 Flo Whyard (editor) *Martha Black* (Formerly *My Ninety Years*), Anchorage: Alaska Northwest Books, 1989, 143.
62 Ibid, 143.
63 Ibid, 146 (interview for Alaska Weekly, 1940)
64 Flo Whyard, Interview for CBC, 1956.
65 Mrs. George Black, *My Seventy Years*, page 108.
66 Flo Whyard (editor) *Martha Black*, 162.
67 Flo Whyard, Interview for CBC, 1956.
68 *Whitehorse Star*, 1957.

RELATED CANADIANA FROM HANCOCK HOUSE

Burnt Snow: My years living & working with the Dene of the Northwest Territories

Moore, Kieran

978-0-88839-100-1 [paperback]
978-0-88839-356-2 [hardcover]
978-0-88839-265-7 [epub]
6 x 9, sc, 272pp
$24.95

The Power of Dreams: 27 years off-grid in a wilderness valley

Dave & Rosemary Neads

978-0-88839-718-8 [paperback]

978-0-88839-742-3 [epub]

5½ x 8½, sc, 246pp

$24.95

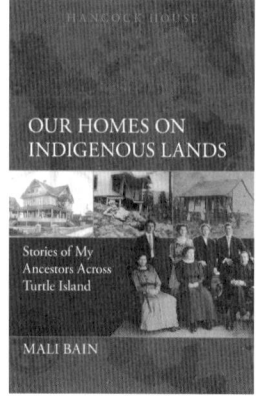

Our Homes on Indigenous Lands: Stories of my Ancestors Across Turtle Island

Bain, Mali

978-0-88839-741-6 [paperback]

978-0-88839-748-5 [epub]

5½ x 8½, sc, 202pp

$24.95

HANCOCK HOUSE PUBLISHERS LTD.
19313 Zero Avenue, Surrey, B.C. Canada V3Z 9R9
#104-4550 Birch Bay-Lynden Rd, Blaine, WA, U.S.A. 98230-9436
(800) 938-1114 Fax (800) 983-2262
www.hancockhouse.com info@hancockhouse.com